You hold in yo

MW01235997

Start here and it's a book for girls aged 12-19. Flip it over and a book for dads. Both of the books cover the same 10 critical conversations that fathers and daughters need to have during the teen years.

As dad and daughter pass this book back and forth, they end up talking about identity, faith, friends, beauty, boys, sex, porn, and their desperate need to stay connected to one another during the teen years. Because they have to share, it forces them to keep the dialogue open about what they are reading and learning.

Finally, the two books literally meet in the middle. In the center of the book, dad and daughter will find a commitment. It's a pledge to stay connected and to offer unconditional love to each other, serving as a constant reminder of how important the father/daughter relationship will always be.

Stay close to your dad. Keep talking to him.

Meet him in the middle.

Barrett and Jenifer Johnson are the founders of I.N.F.O. for Families, a ministry committed to helping Imperfect and Normal Families navigate our hyper-sexualized culture. The authors of *The Talks* and *The Young Man's Guide to Awesomeness*, they have raised five kids (including three daughters) and have been married for 28 years.

www.INFOforFamilies.com

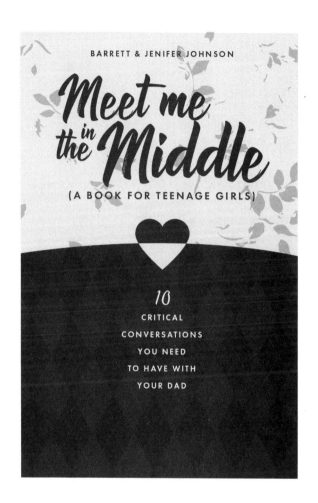

BARRETT & JENIFER JOHNSON

Meet me in the Middle

(A BOOK FOR TEENAGE GIRLS)

10
CRITICAL
CONVERSATIONS
YOU NEED
TO HAVE WITH
YOUR DAD

Also from Barrett and Jenifer Johnson:

The Talks

Your Imperfect & Normal Family

The Young Man's Guide to Awesomeness

INFO FOR FAMILIES resources

Meet Me in the Middle

An I.N.F.O. for Families Resource

www.INFOforFamilies.com

Printed in the United States of America

ISBN: 978-0-692-15302-4

Cover Design by Lucas Bauer.

For Lindsey, Emilie, and Maddie Kate.

May you always desire to walk with your heavenly Father, in spite of the imperfect example you had in your earthly one.

Contents

Introduction

Hi, there!

If you're reading these words right now, it's because you're a girl. If you're not a girl, then you're in the wrong place. If you happen to be a dad, you can flip the book over and start there. If you are neither a dad nor a girl, then go read something else. There's nothing for you here.

Just so you know from the start, we have written this book to help you navigate some issues that many girls struggle with. They are topics that we think are universal. Even if you haven't encountered them yet, it's likely that you will deal with this stuff at some point.

This book is also designed to help you to connect with your father. While there are times you might think he is a bit clueless about the things you face, he actually might be able to help you. During the teenage years when many girls pull away from their fathers, we would suggest that it is the season when you need him the most. That's why we created this tool to encourage some meaningful conversations between you and your dad.

If you haven't already noticed, what you're holding right now is actually two books. One is for you and one is for your dad. They both cover the same content, but they come at it from two different perspectives: what you need to know and what your dad needs to know.

Because it's two books in one, you and your dad are going to have to share. You should read a chapter and then let your dad read the corresponding chapter in his book. Then you have to get together and talk about it.

We called this thing *Meet Me in the Middle* for a couple of reasons.

The first is because we know that dads and daughters can sometimes have a hard time finding neutral ground to connect. If you're going to stay close to him during this season, you're going to have to "meet him in the middle" and get into his world a bit. You're going to have to make an attempt to see things from your dad's perspective.

And don't worry. In the book for dads, we're telling him to do the exact same thing, encouraging him to see things from your viewpoint.

The other reason we called this book *Meet Me in the Middle* is because of the way the two books are laid out. If you notice, both of you start from your end and then your reading eventually takes you to the middle of the book.

Once you are all done, we encourage you to make the commitment that you find there. But there's no rush. You'll get there eventually.

As you read, you'll see *a whole bunch of quotes in bold type*. These are direct quotes from some 20-something young women that we know. These are incredibly valuable insights from some girls who have already made it through their teenage years.

Trust us, they have some really good things to say. See them as wise big sisters who care about you and who want you to make it through adolescence with your head screwed on straight.

One more thing: this is not just a static "read the words" book like you typically have in school. It's meant to be interactive. Take advantage of the suggested activities and discussion starters to help you to connect with your dad. Feel free to scribble in the margins any thoughts you might want to share with him. Don't just read this book. Experience it!

We sincerely hope that working through this resource with your dad will help you to gain God's perspective on a bunch of stuff you're likely dealing with. We also hope you have fun spending time with the old man.

Hopefully, you'll find God's design for your life to be incredibly satisfying. In addition, you'll remember that your dad is a pretty good guy after all.

-Barrett and Jenifer Johnson

1

Your Dad

A much-loved TV series about family relationships has taken the U.S. by storm over the past few years. "This is Us" is unique in that it simultaneously shows the lives of two generations within the same family. By carefully weaving these two stories together, "This is Us" reminds us that where we come from matters. Simply put, the key events of your childhood will potentially stay with you for life.

In the case of the Pearson family, Kate stands out as a pivotal character. She is the lone daughter within a set of triplets. While her brothers have gone on to success in adulthood, she is still trying to find her way. She also has a severe weight problem. Through all of this, her relationship with her dad is perhaps the most emotionally powerful one on the show.

Even though she pushed back on her dad at times, his

unconditional love for her during her teen years provided a much-needed anchor in her life. While her relationship with her mom was often tense, dad was a consistent affirmation to her. She didn't realize his importance until he died during her senior year of high school. Much of the show is devoted to her "flashbacks" to what he did and said to her during her developmental years. (Heads up: here's the first piece of advice from the young women we told you about.)

"In the midst of life's drama, your dad's unemotional and logical perspective can be very valuable to you."

"This is Us" illustrates something very real and true: dads matter. Kate didn't fully realize that until she reached adulthood and found herself trying to navigate her life without him around. Know this: YOUR dad matters. If you get anything out of this book, we hope that you learn this lesson sooner than later.

WHY YOUR RELATIONSHIP WITH YOUR DAD MATTERS

Many people say that the teen years are the best of your life. If you are like most girls, it sure doesn't feel that way when you're in the middle of it.

As you move through the tumultuous waters of adolescence, there will be many days (and months and years) when you won't know which way is up. The hormonal and physical changes your body is going through will do a number on you. Your brain will find itself focusing much of its energy on where you stand in your social relationships, in your family, and in God's big picture.

You may not fully buy into this, but your dad can help you to find your way. He may not fully grasp all that you are going through, but it could be that an occasionally clueless but usually consistent and experienced older man is just what you need. For most girls, dad is the perfect guy for the job.

"When my dad tells me stories and I actually take time to listen, I usually learn something."

Girls seek male approval just as boys want the admiration of the women in their lives. And it all starts with dad. It is a special bond like no other. If the relationship you have with your dad is solid, it has the power to be the most important and influential one in your life. If your dad makes you feel loved, valuable, intelligent, and beautiful, then you are likely to believe you are, in spite of all the other messages the world throws at you. Granted, you may doubt it at times, but if dad's voice is consistent, it's the sort of stuff that sticks with you for life.

THE LIE YOU ARE LED TO BELIEVE

As you move through your teenage years, a lot of different sources will begin to tell you a lie. Both the media you ingest and many of the friends you interact with will tell you the same thing: "Your dad is clueless." This is the attitude of many teen girls, so it's tempting to accept it as truth.

You are likely to begin to believe that your dad is irrelevant. That he can't possibly understand what you are going through. That he can't relate. The ironic thing is that as you begin to experience more "adult" issues, you are likely to start thinking that your dad – one of the key adults in your life – doesn't have anything to offer.

"Your dad really cares about you! He just doesn't always know how to show it."

Why do so many teenage girls get the wrong idea that their dads no longer matter? It's because so many dads do, in fact, check out during a season when they are needed more than ever. Their daughters become too complicated, too emotional, and too dramatic. When you start changing physically and are no longer daddy's little girl, he gets a bit freaked out. The result is that connecting with your dad used to be easy and now it's a challenge. (For the record, he's not the only one to blame. It is likely that you have unintentionally made it a bit hard on him.)

The net result of all of this is that most girls buy into the lie that dad has nothing to offer you. When, in fact, he does. But that's the attitude of most girls. It's not going to be you.

THE ACTUAL TRUTH

People will come in and out of your life. There will be friends, classmates, co-workers, and thousands of other people who you will connect with on social media.

In the midst of all your shallow relationships, you will forge relationships with a few key people whose impact on your life will stay with you forever. Your dad falls into that category.

Even if he isn't always present or if he dies younger than you expect, his impact will continue to be felt in your life.

He does matter. How he sees you, how he loves you, how he treats you.... all of these things have the power to impact how you feel about yourself. And couldn't we all use a bit of encouragement during adolescence, the most difficult season of our lives?

"Your parents will always be your biggest cheerleaders. Don't harm that relationship by being a jerk to them."

Granted, because of their father's negative influence, many girls have a terrible experience during their teen years. Their dad is absent, emotionally disconnected, or, at worst, critical and unloving. That happens to many. Let's be honest: most dads don't have a clue what they are doing. They don't know how to love and lead a teenage girl. But you can help him. The fact that he is willing to read this book with you shows that he wants to get it right. That willingness can go a long way if you will let it.

God wants to help you. The very last verse in the Old Testament is Malachi 4:6. It gives a prophecy about the ministry of a new messenger from God who *"will turn the hearts of fathers to their children, and the hearts of children to their fathers."* When all has been said and done in the old covenant, this is how God chooses to wrap things up.

Then, after four hundred years of silence, at the very beginning of the New Testament, we see another reference to this messenger. In Luke 1:17, it similarly says that he will *"turn the hearts of the fathers to their children, and he will cause those who are rebellious to accept the wisdom of the godly."*

If the Old Testament ends with this theme and the New Testament opens with it, then it might be worth noting what God is trying to tell us. He is suggesting that the father/child relationship is critical to experiencing God's best in our lives. In other words, dads and daughters have to stay close to one another. In a culture where teenage girls tend to discount their dads (and distance themselves from them) you have to work hard to stay close. God knows that you need him.

"It really helps if you humble yourself. The time will soon come when you realize that you don't have it all figured out."

HOW YOU CAN BE DIFFERENT

What can you start doing to foster the right kind of relationship with your dad? How can you connect with him when many of your friends are checking out on their dads? Here are a few places to start:

1. Give Your Dad a Break

One thing that kids often forget about their parents is that children don't come with instruction manuals. Unless you are daughter #7 in a family of 12, your dad doesn't have much experience parenting teenage girls. In many ways, he is making it up as he goes along. So it would help if you cut him some slack. In fact, you would do well to give him tons of bonus points for effort.

"Remember that, like you, your dad is just figuring this out. He is going to make some mistakes."

There is one thing he has experience with: life. He has already made the transition into adulthood. He has been there and done that. He has experience with friendships and school and some of the major decisions that you are going to face in the next decade. So maybe he isn't as oblivious as you think he is. In fact, many young people end up saying, "The older I get, the more I realize that my parents were right."

2. Remember that Cool is Over-rated

Unless your father is a male model or an avid reader of GQ magazine, he probably isn't the coolest guy on the planet. His jokes are often lame. His taste in music is terrible. His fashion choices are probably questionable at times. Still, you need to keep reminding yourself that these things do not matter in the grand scheme of things. They don't matter at all.

You don't need cool. You need dad. This key man in your life can offer the things you need at this season of life, even if he is a nerd of epic proportions. So while it's okay to choose friends that fit your version of "cool," you don't get to choose your dad. And that's okay. God gave you the wonderful, but nerdy, wise, yet goofy guy that He gave you for a reason. As you work to show him what you need from him, your prayer is that he will be teachable. Cool is irrelevant.

3. Ask Him For Permission to Be Honest

There is one key place where many father/daughter relationships are compromised. It is when daughters are honest with their feelings and their dads bring judgment or say that those particular feelings are not acceptable or allowed. You want to be able to share what you are experiencing and feeling with your dad, so you may need to ask him if you can be blunt. This includes any perspectives you have that might hurt his feelings. Always stay respectful and gentle, but ask for permission to be honest.

Transparency about how things really are (even if the truth hurts) is the key to relational connection. Dads are often terrible at this. Because men have the natural tendency to be defensive or to be "fixers," your dad won't always know how to respond to your raw and ugly honesty. This is one key area where you will need to teach him.

"We girls have a fear of letting people in and being vulnerable. We don't like to show our weakness and insecurities. Be brave and let your dad in on these things."

Let him know that if he responds in a way that feels to you like he is withholding love, it will be harder to share in the future. In contrast, if he accepts your feelings and perspectives just as they are, with no judgment, then it makes it easier to bring your struggles to him. You will come to know him as a safe place to turn when times are tough. If you can come to an agreement with him about this issue, it will be a key to building and maintaining a strong relationship with him.

MEET YOUR DAD IN THE MIDDLE

Start becoming a student of your dad. Pay attention to how he interacts with others, what he loves, and what he does apart from his relationship with you. This will help you to understand him better. As you start reading this book together, it might feel a bit strange to have the intentional conversations suggested here. Try to push through the awkwardness to make it happen. Carve out some time to go on a walk or a date together just to start talking.

SOME THINGS TO TALK ABOUT

*Tell your dad about the sort of relationships that your friends have with their dads. Which ones aren't so hot? Which ones do you envy and why?

*Describe what the "ideal" relationship with him might look like. Ask him to tell you what he thinks it would look like.

* Be sure to bring up the "honesty" issue mentioned above.

*Affirm the good things you see in your dad and why you value him in your life.

2

Friends

Depending on your age, you're likely in a season of life where everything is changing. Think about it. As you move from childhood towards adulthood, your body, your mind, and your relationships are shifting in more significant ways than at any other stage of your life. That's why the teen years are so hard for many girls.

One of the markers of adolescence is pulling away from home. Over about 10 years of time, you slowly but surely gain more and more independence. The opinions of your friends become more important to you and the perspectives of your parents become less important. (This swings back the other way once you get into your twenties.)

For now, the relationships you have with your friends are important, but they are not without risk and pain. In fact, adolescent girls in their natural environment can be some of the cruelest people on the planet. Unfortunately, you're probably going to have to interact with these people every day.

Teenage girls have the power to bring hurt and suffering to each other like nothing else in our culture. Of course, they aren't murderers and they rarely cause any physical pain, but the emotional wounds that girls can inflict on each other can feel incredibly real and raw. Add to that the fact that adolescence is one of the most tender and emotionally fragile seasons of a your life, and it's a very big deal.

"Girls wrongly think that everyone else is fine and that they are the only ones struggling. The truth is that everyone is insecure."

Few girls escape this season unscathed, including you. Even if you have a tough exterior and a confident personality, you are still likely to be wounded by your friends. If you're not willing to face these relationships with a measure of maturity, you're going to suffer.

WHY DEALING WITH YOUR FRIENDS MATTERS

The time will probably come when you will look back on your teenage years and all the girl drama you had to endure. You will likely look back and think, "It was foolish for me to care so much about what my friends thought about me." But that's for later. Now, what you feel about this stuff is real. For many girls, it is the most real thing in their lives. Because isolating yourself on a deserted island until you are 21 isn't an option, you're going to have to learn to navigate your "friend" relationships.

"You are going to be lonely at times. But being alone isn't such a bad deal. You will get through it."

It's going to require a measure of perspective about what is really going on. As you make the transition from childhood to adulthood, you're going to have to discover who you are, not in the context of your family, but in the larger world out there. While you will hopefully – and eventually -- find the answer to that question in God's eyes, for now, you are likely to look to your friends.

What makes that near impossible is that your friends are a fickle, clueless, and unreliable bunch. While you are comparing yourself to others and seeking significance and worth from your peer group, each of your friends is doing the exact same thing. It's like there's a big competition going on and the cruelest people in the bunch are constantly changing the rules.

The unfortunate result for you is that what your friends say about you, how you fit in, and where you land in the social order all have the power to define your reality. In many cases, your friends are the voices you hear the loudest and they can be very, very persuasive, even if they are a bunch of stupid girls.

THE LIE YOU ARE LED TO BELIEVE

While teenagers from every generation have had to deal with "mean girls," smartphones have multiplied their impact. Hard as this is to believe, your dad and mom typically went home from school in the afternoon and didn't talk to most of their friends again until lunchtime at school the next day. In contrast, the smartphone generation has never known what it is like to interact with their friends apart from texting and social media. This is huge.

The constant connection you have with your friends means that they will have constant influence on your life. While there is a temptation to declare this as "awesome," you need to understand that this is a bad thing. Because, again, most of the people you are interacting with online are not looking out for your best interests. They are looking out for themselves and they really don't care if you get hurt in the process.

There is a lie that many girls buy into. They believe what the phone in their pocket says about them. In the course of any given day, most girls will send and receive hundreds of texts, be tagged in dozens of pictures, and check their phones for social media updates 50 to 100 times a day. They are subconsciously looking for clues to their value. Sadly, these girls may even think that they actually have 1,250 friends. The entire system is a disaster.

Since your friends -- including the mean ones -- have access to the same platforms, it's a free-for-all. Anyone can say anything to anybody. Even the "tagging" feature on social media can be a form of bullying. One friend might post a picture of a group and then tag some of the girls (her way of saying "look at us!") but not include others. It's a purposeful slam that you have probably felt at some point along the way.

"Social media makes you think that everybody is together all the time. They aren't."

This desire to fit in and be included (FOMO, or the Fear Of

Missing Out) is commonly found at the center of the teenage girl's brain. But just because it is there, it doesn't mean that it's healthy. Give it too much focus and energy, and you're setting yourself up for a miserable adolescence. There's nothing wrong with wanting to hang out with people, but some girls get obsessed over it.

THE ACTUAL TRUTH

In the midst of trying to fit in with their friends, many girls forget that their worth and value is not found in the opinions of others. In spite of how important those relationships might seem, the truth is that they matter very little in the grand scheme of things. Instead of putting your energy into being loved and affirmed by others, true and meaningful relationships are formed when you focus on loving and affirming the people around you.

During this challenging season of difficult (and sometimes cruel) friendships, you would be wise to find stability in those people whom you know you can trust. Start with your relationship with God. Instead of looking to the affirmations of others on your phone in the form of follows, likes, clicks, and comments, believe that God loves you fully regardless of what you do.

With regard to your parents – and particularly your dad – you need to have confidence that they are there for you. This can be hard because your relationship with your father can sometimes feel so awkward. But it's okay to tell him that you need to know that he is in your corner. In a time when everyone else seems to be completely unreliable, you need a strong, stable force of love in your life. Dad might not always show it well, but he can be this for you.

Girl drama can be pretty ugly, but you will get through it. You will one day come out the other side with a heart that is not quite as impacted by the opinions of your friends. Unfortunately, you're going to have to endure it for a few years. Keeping the truly faithful people in your life close by can help you to get through it. When you make an effort to lean into your dad's love, the payoff is usually awesome.

In Galatians 1:10, Paul asks a rhetorical question. With his strong personality and blunt writing, you can be sure that he is making an important point. He asks, *"Am I now trying to win the approval of human beings, or of God? Or am I trying to please people?"*

Paul suggests that striving for the approval of other people will almost always lead to disappointment. And even if you were to pull it off and be incredibly popular with everyone, you're probably not doing it by pleasing God. You can't have both.

You can also be sure that where God is always reliable, your friends (no matter how great they are) will eventually let you down. Proverbs 18:24 says, *"One who has unreliable friends soon comes to ruin, but there is a friend who sticks closer than a brother."* It's hard to comprehend this, but some of your best, closest friends now might not even be in your life in two or three years.

"Finding that one good friend is a beautiful thing."

Through it all, know that God will consistently be there. So will your father. Flawed as he is, your dad will probably be a significant part of your story for the bulk of your life. That's why it's so important for you to stay connected to him, even during a season where it takes more work.

HOW YOU CAN BE DIFFERENT

If you hope to maintain your sanity while navigating all the erratic friendships in your life, you're going to have to do a few things. Here's where to start:

1. Be Yourself

Striving to "fit in" by becoming what everyone else thinks you should be can be absolutely exhausting. It can also lead you to compromise your principles and become something of a jerk. Get comfortable in your own skin and then bring that person to your relationships. There is nothing wrong with wanting to be loved, but desiring popularity at all costs will often result in some very bad things.

2. Be A Good Friend

It is a given that a few "mean girls" will be particularly cruel and vicious during your teen years. Unfortunately, the vast majority of other girls will get caught up in their drama and go along with it. What your group of friends needs is someone who will lay their insecurities aside and step up to be kind, generous, and selfless. This could be you.

> *"That love and care that you are looking for in others? Be that to somebody. Stop making friendships all about you."*

Look for those people who need love the most. Then love them. These will probably be girls who are not popular and who will not improve your social status, but who cares? Jesus talked an awful lot about loving *"the least of these,"* so when you go out of your way to be nice to people who aren't at the top of the social ladder, you are obeying a simple command of God. He will honor you for it.

3. Believe What God Has Said About You

There are plenty of voices telling you who you are and what value you have, but only One voice truly matters. Listen to God on this, not your friends. Your friends may be good people, but they are still unreliable. Only God's voice speaks the truth and only God's opinion has any weight. (There will be more on this in the next chapter.)

HOW YOUR DAD CAN HELP

Your dad will probably have some idea of the impact that friend drama has on your life. He is probably also aware that your smartphone is making it worse. If that's true, then you need to welcome any parameters he wants to put on your use of social media. If he asks to "follow you" on the apps you use, or if he asks to look at your phone occasionally, don't see that as a threat. See it as his desire to guard and protect you. That's what dads are wired to do. And you need that.

Also, if you share your friend drama with your dad, he's going to be tempted to "fix it." He will want to work the problem and give you a solution to your relationship problems. Encourage him not to do this.

Teach him to just listen and offer compassion and understanding. But know that he might be able to help you brainstorm some possible solutions of how to work through a problem, so use him for that, as well.

MEET YOUR DAD IN THE MIDDLE

Talk to your dad honestly about some of the challenging relationships in your life. Because guys are far less dramatic, he may not be able to fully relate to your experiences. Still, he needs to know what you face. Look to him for encouragement and believe him if he tells you that you're going to eventually get through it.

SOME THINGS TO TALK ABOUT

*Talk about how social media might make you feel insecure or cause you to experience FOMO.

*Share honestly about how much time your brain spends thinking about friend relationships and your place in your social world. Has that changed over the past few years for the better or the worse?

*Brainstorm some ways that you both can be good friends to some people at school or work or in your neighborhood that need to be shown the love of Jesus.

3

Identity

Every person in our culture lives in a constant state of comparison. We compare our looks, our stuff, our grades, our performance, our accomplishments, and just about everything else that our modern society offers.

The scorecards are different for the various arenas of life. Some, like our grades in school or our income in the workplace, are tangible. Some are less clear, like our social status or our looks. Sadly, social media has enabled what used to be abstract to become much more concrete. As we move further and further into lives defined by "likes" and "follows," girls like you will suffer more and more.

The Netflix series Black Mirror characterized this beautifully in an episode called "Nosedive." In the near future where status is clearly tracked and scored online, a woman's life collapses when she can't earn enough points to climb the social ladder as she wishes. It was a troubling show to watch, but it seemed somehow familiar. The awful future it showed is the future we are headed for.

From the time you were little, you have been subconsciously trying to find your place in the world. How you fit in with your friends dictates much about how you feel about yourself. Because of the technology you are so comfortable with, you constantly compare yourself to others, trying to measure yourself based upon unrealistic ideals of success, happiness, beauty, and popularity. It's exhausting.

> *"There will be days you won't like yourself. That's okay. Just don't do anything stupid. You've got to learn to see yourself as God sees you."*

But it gets worse. Because your life is lived out on social media, your so-called social "shortcomings" are there for everyone to see. No matter how popular you might be, there are times when you will end up feeling inadequate at best and bullied at worst. You are in desperate need to find your identity in something bigger than what your friends say about you.

WHY WHO YOU ARE MATTERS

Throughout your childhood, the main messages you hear are that you are pretty, kind, and valuable. Hopefully, your dad has affirmed these things in you. You might have some internal doubts, but you likely believed these things to be true because they were the primary messages your parents gave you every day. Then you entered the 6th grade.

All the work your parents did to build up your self-esteem

begins to be undermined in middle school. Unfortunately, this is the season that most girls like you become introduced to their first smartphone. Add to that the hormonal powder keg that is your mind and body and it's a toxic combination.

During these years, you are bombarded with messages that run contrary to the narrative you have heard for the first part of your life. Cruel and insensitive people begin to say things that suggest you are ugly, lame, stupid, or that you just don't measure up. You aren't good enough.

This is why it is critical that you have a clear sense of your identity: who God says you are. In a noisy season of life where many voices are telling you what you are worth, you need to hear the message that God wants to speak over you. If you don't listen for God, your tender heart can easily believe the nonsense that the world is screaming at you.

"Own who you are. Don't care so much about what people think of you."

THE LIE YOU ARE LED TO BELIEVE

In hundreds of different forms, you are going to hear the lie that has been spoken to humanity since the serpent first spoke it to Adam. The fundamental lie is that God is not enough for you. You need more than Him to find your worth. While his lie takes on many forms, your mind is likely to believe one of several versions of it.

In his groundbreaking book, *The Search for Significance*, author Robert McGee summarizes the lie into four things, all of which are rooted in our wrong belief that our self worth is based upon our performance and the opinions of others. The lies he writes about are:

1. The Performance Trap:
"I must meet certain standards to feel good about myself."

2. The Approval Addict:
"I must be approved by certain others to feel good about myself."

3. The Blame Game:
"Those who fail are unworthy of love and deserve to be punished."

4. Shame:
"I am what I am. I cannot change. I am hopeless."

Just about every struggle you face during your teen years can be traced back to the first three lies listed above. Peer pressure, temptation, identity crises, and just about anything else adolescent girls go through are rooted in these things. If you are unable to embrace God's truth about who you are, you might come to believe lie #4 about shame.

This is not God's desire for you. God desperately wants you to know all that He has done to rescue you from these lies.

THE ACTUAL TRUTH

Perhaps the biggest milestone in your spiritual life will occur when you grasp who you are in Christ. When you come to believe the truth about who God says you are, you can reject all the lies that others try to throw your way. This is key to finding your place in God's big story, because it's hard to be confident in who God has made you to be if you're paying too much attention to what everyone else is saying.

"What you get from others will be inconsistent. Know where the consistent truth will come from: only God. Your parents might help, but even they will let you down."

Doing this truly requires that you turn your heart and mind towards God. It starts with loving Him, but it can't end there. You're going to have to learn to hear His voice and follow His leading in your life. Unfortunately, this rarely happens by just going to church. It requires you to truly believe that He is everything.

Many girls never fall in love with Jesus and find Him to be altogether satisfying. And this is where they go wrong. They have this intense longing to connect, to be needed, and to be loved. But these are all longings that only God can satisfy. Most girls bypass their Creator (God) and look to the created (other people) to get their deepest needs met.

Eventually, they will look to a man to meet that need. They will stand at an altar, making their vows, pledging their lives and their futures to their grooms. If they haven't first found their identity in Christ, what these girls are really saying to their future husbands is this: "I'm counting on you to 'complete me.' I'm depending on you to give me my identity and my meaning in life. I'm counting on you to meet my every need."

This fundamental worth and purpose and identity can

never be found in another person. It can only be found in the person of Jesus Christ. You have value because of who your Creator says you are. Only when you embrace this can you begin to develop a healthy and lasting self-image.

So who are you, really? Who has God made you to be? What does He say about you? While you can find answers to these questions throughout the Bible, there are a few key verses that clearly define your identity. Once you start believing that these things are true of you at the core of your being, everything will change in your interactions with others. (It would be a great idea to look these verses up, find ones that speak to you, and write them down someplace you can regularly see them.) As a child of Christ, you...

- Are God's child (John 1:12)

- Are Christ's friend (John 15:15)

- Belong to God (I Corinthian 6:19-20)

- Are a saint; a holy one (Ephesians 1:1)

- Are free from condemnation (Romans 8:1-2)

- Cannot be separated from God's love (Romans 8:35-39)

- Have been redeemed and forgiven (Colossians 1:14)

- Are a citizen of Heaven (Philippians 3:20)

- Can approach God with confidence (Ephesians 3:12)

- Are complete in Christ (Colossians 2:10)

This is who you are! You don't have to earn it or hope for it.

Because of Jesus, those who have trusted in Him have been given spiritual birth as children of God. This is your new identity! If other people say things that contradict the truth of God, you can know that they are telling you a lie.

"Up to a point in my life, I lived my life wanting acceptance and affirmation from other people. Then God changed everything when I realized that God defined my worth when He made me his child. Now nothing else matters."

HOW YOU CAN BE DIFFERENT

With all the bad information out there about your worth and value, you're going to have to work your entire life to truly embrace what God has said about you. There are a few ways to begin to develop this discipline:

1. Be Mindful of Wrong Thinking

In 2 Corinthians 10:5, you are instructed to *"take every thought captive to the obedience of Christ."* That's bible-speak for "constantly evaluate the thoughts you have to see if they are from God." Much of your thoughts about yourself during this season of life will be lies from the enemy delivered by your friends. If you are feeling worthless or inadequate, BE CERTAIN that it is not God talking to you.

Comparison will do a huge number on you during those times you feel you don't measure up in some situation. And nothing is more awful than when you are left out of something. It's easy to enter into a state of "I'm so lonely and nobody loves me." When you sense these feelings coming over you, take a moment to pray, asking God to remind you of who He says you are. Negative thoughts are common, but it doesn't mean you have to dwell on them.

2. Cut Yourself Some Slack

One thing that might help you is to lower your standards for perfection and performance a bit. It could be that you are expecting far too much out of yourself. In a 2018 MTV Movie award speech, Chris Pratt gave some great advice about this. Here's what he said:

"Nobody is perfect. People are going to tell you that you're perfect just the way you are. You're not. You are imperfect. You always will be. But, there is a powerful force that designed you that way. If you are willing to accept that, you will have grace. And grace is a gift...and that gift was paid for with someone else's blood. Do not forget it. Don't take it for granted."

When you fully recognize (and embrace) your imperfections, you realize your desperate need for Jesus. Only then can He begin the process of re-making you into His image the way that He wants to.

3. When You Fail, Remember Who You Are

When you screw up in a big way (in school or in a relationship or with your parents) remember that the screw up does not define who you are. Only God can do that. There may be a consequence or a punishment from your parents, but don't allow the "blame game" lie sneak into your mind.

Just remember that what you did is not who you are meant to be. Believe the truth of who God has made you to be in

Christ. Embrace your identity as a new creation that is being slowly grown into the image of Jesus. "This is who I am...God help me to start acting like it." The verses mentioned earlier can remind you of these things.

HOW YOUR DAD CAN HELP

Do you remember all those cheesy things your dad told you as a little girl? "You're beautiful. You're smart. You're loved. You're my princess." As silly as those things can seem, you need to know that your dad is still right. In a subconscious way, he was joining God in His holy efforts to remind you of exactly who you are and how precious you are to Him.

If and when your dad still says those things, don't be a dork and push him away. Don't ignore his words of affirmation and praise. You need to hear them from your earthly father because they are just a small taste of what your Heavenly Father wants to tell you. And if your dad doesn't say things like that to you any more, it's okay to ask him to. Remind him that you're still daddy's girl.

MEET YOUR DAD IN THE MIDDLE

Have a talk with your dad about the power of his words. Let him know how his words can sometimes hurt you. Also, be willing to tell him that you still need to hear his words of encouragement. Ask him what things you might do or say to encourage or discourage him in his role as dad.

SOME THINGS TO TALK ABOUT

*Ask your dad to reflect back on his teen years. Did he ever struggle with feelings of inadequacy or insecurity?

*Openly share some of the ways you see yourself when you look in a mirror. Share some of the negative things that your friends sometimes make you feel about yourself. Give your dad some tips on how he can help counteract those feelings.

*Read through the list of truths about your identity in Christ from a few pages back. Ask your dad if he has any problems believing those things about himself.

4

Beauty

The start of the average girl's day hasn't changed much in the past 50 years. She wakes up, does her hair and makeup, gets dressed, has a quick breakfast and then heads out the door for school. But in the past 10 years, an extra layer of pressure has been added to the average girl's burden to look "nice."

At some point during her day, someone is likely to take her picture. It may be the selfies she shoots or the pictures her friends post on Instagram or a few quick clips on Snapchat. While photos were relatively rare even 15 years ago, smartphones make pictures (and the burden of looking cute) a common thing.

Because there is immediate feedback, every picture that a girl posts on social media is a risk. She is tempted to evaluate her worth as an individual based upon how many people "like" her image in the odd scoring system our world has created. She subconsciously looks to her friends or the boys she knows for affirmation. If she doesn't get it, it's devastating. Unfortunately, if she gets affirmation via tons of "likes," she starts believing the lie that her friends have the power to define her beauty.

> *"Try to look nice, but stop looking to social media to tell you that you look good. Just stop."*

This longing to be affirmed clearly illustrates the private, internal conflict that most girls wrestle with. It seems to be hard-wired into the female brain to want to know the answer to this question: "Am I pretty?" Sadly, during the awkward teen years when your body is constantly changing, it can show up as one of the central themes of your subconscious brain. You could probably use a little help in managing it.

WHY YOUR UNDERSTANDING OF BEAUTY MATTERS

News flash: there are a few dozen supermodels who are setting the pace for what is beautiful in our culture. Also living on our planet are three billion other women who are NOT supermodels. They are normal people who don't have personal trainers and dieticians and stylists and Photoshop to make them look perfect. Sadly, the standard that the supermodels set for what is beautiful is totally unrealistic.

Add to that the problem that our world's definition of beauty is constantly changing. One year, curvy is pretty. A few years later, it's extra skinny. The powers that be can easily roll out some new models that fit the standard, but the average girl out there will never be able to keep up. Hear this: YOU will never be able to keep up.

For that reason, it is essential that you gain, and then maintain, a healthy view of your beauty. You need to embrace the fact that it is based on far more than how your appearance compares with others. There is certainly nothing wrong with spending some time working on your looks, but what you really need is a God-given perspective of the fact that you are "wonderfully made." This belief and confidence has the power to sustain you as fashion trends shift and change.

THE LIE YOU ARE LED TO BELIEVE

There is a subtle message that is constantly being whispered to the girls of your generation: your appearance is what matters most. While this has been true for young women through the ages, there has been a major shift in the past decade. Today, being beautiful has been surpassed by the greater value of being "sexy."

"If someone is critical of how you look, they are doing it just to be mean. They won't think about it later."

The "role models" that your friends are following tend to sell this brand of beauty. Sadly, many girls are buying what these celebrities are selling.

Consider the Kardashians. Before they got famous for being famous, what was their creative or cultural or intellectual contribution to society? Anyone? Their brand and the bulk of their influence are based almost entirely on their sex appeal. Their Instagram accounts are filled almost entirely with selfies, and nearly 250 million people are watching their every move.

As many girls transition into womanhood, it is likely that the question they are asking has shifted from, "Am I pretty" to, "Am I sexy?" If you scan the Instagram accounts of most teenage girls today, you will likely see the same pouty faces and alluring poses that you see on the filtered photos of Kim, Khloe and Kourtney. And I guarantee that what these girls check over and over again are the comment sections of their photos. What are people saying? Are they answering the question that they are crying out for the answer to: "How do I look?"

If you are using social media to answer that question, something needs to change. The built in scorecard of likes and comments is a terrible source of truth. On most days, you will be left with discouragement and frustration. You will come to believe that you not pretty enough. Or, even worse, that what people say about you actually matters. News flash: it doesn't.

THE ACTUAL TRUTH

When you were a little girl, you had no reason to doubt that you were pretty. The voices you mainly heard -- mom and dad – assured you of that reality. When you asked them for their opinions, you were likely looking for an affirmation of what you already knew to be true. "Yes, dad... I know.... I'm beautiful."

But something happens during the transition to the teen years. You stop believing the truth that you are wonderfully made and start buying into the lie that says you will never measure up. The comparison trap will get you every time, because there will always be someone who is prettier or who gets more attention for their looks.

That's why a healthy self-image is so important. It's the belief that God has wisely made you in His image. That image has a soul and a heart and a character that is so much more complex than simply external appearance. One thing that you must come to embrace during this season is that a healthy self-image has the power to trump our world's idea of beauty. One is temporary and the other will sustain you for life.

> *"Learn how to love yourself. Nobody teaches you how to do that."*

Scripture can seem to give two contrary views about the value of a woman's beauty. On the one hand, Psalm 144:12b encourages a father to take pride in his daughter's beauty. The psalmist writes, *"Our daughters will be like pillars carved to adorn a palace."* There is nothing wrong with celebrating the femininity that God has blessed you with.

On the other hand, God warns us not to prioritize external beauty over the character of the heart. In I Peter 3:3-4, women are commanded, *"Don't be concerned about the outward beauty of fancy hairstyles, expensive jewelry, or beautiful clothes. You should clothe yourselves instead with the beauty that comes from within, the unfading beauty of a gentle and quiet spirit, which is so precious to God."* Hear this critical point: it is what is inside of you that is the most beautiful.

Both of these perspectives are found in Scripture, so both are true. The challenge you will face is in finding a healthy balance. Sure, it is hard to downplay the importance of external beauty when every voice around you screams that it matters most, especially when some of the voices are quite loud. The challenge is to ignore the voices that say that your looks define you. For it is just not true. You are so much more that that.

HOW YOU CAN BE DIFFERENT

1. Guard Social Media

Every time you post a selfie, you are taking a risk. You may be simply looking for some positive affirmation, but there is always the possibility that you will get a cruel comment from someone who wants to hurt you. Or you may hear "crickets," which might have an altogether different effect on your self-esteem.

No generation before yours has had a system in place that so opens girls up to emotional harm. Your smartphone can be a terrific tool but the social media tools that you enjoy can be a huge source of pain. Many researchers even think that the recent increase in teen depression can be traced directly to social media interaction.

> *"Everyone is so insecure and focused on what everyone is thinking about them. But nobody will ever notice your imperfections near as much as you do."*

If that's true (and it probably is), then you need to guard how much time you spend on social media. You need to insulate yourself from letting what others say about you define who you are or how you feel about yourself.

2. Know that Beauty is More Than What's on the Outside

Believing that you are *"fearfully and wonderfully made"* by a God who loves you is a great place to start growing your self-confidence. You can be comfortable in your own skin, even if you don't measure up to the world's unrealistic standard of beauty. You can also focus on the inner parts of your life that make you attractive.

Personal confidence, simple joy, kindness towards others, Christ-like character.... all of these things are beautiful traits that can spill out of a young woman and onto the people around her. When these attributes are nurtured and on display in your life, an undeniable beauty will also be present. The work you put into becoming that sort of person will be time well-spent.

3. Don't Try to Be "Sexy"

Much of what is in fashion today has been created to be "sexy" or "flirty." More simply put, it has been designed to draw the attention of guys. While that may be a temptation, try not to settle for it. It is easy for a girl to dress up her beauty in a way that makes guys notice, but the guys of real substance whom you want to attract will eventually notice you for something more than just how you look.

The substantive beauty that is mentioned in I Peter 3:4 is the kind that gets better over time long after "sexy" loses its steam. Make it your goal to be that sort of woman. Look for older women in your life who are becoming more beautiful with age and strive to be like them.

HOW YOUR DAD CAN HELP

When it comes to how you look and how you dress, your dad might occasionally have to "police" your clothing choices. He knows far more about the male brain than you do, and he probably wants guys to notice you for more than just your outsides.

This is a terrible reality of the world we live in, but when a man sees a woman's skin (or her cleavage or a glimpse of her underwear or anything else that is sexual in nature), his mind has a hard time focusing on anything else.

Sadly, your dad can probably relate to this, so listen to his counsel. He wants you to be a person that guys truly see, not just a body to gaze at. So if he has some direction to give you about how you dress, receive it as an example of his love and care, not just as him being mean.

Also, when your dad affirms your beauty or your character, believe what he says about you. He knows that the world might give you some discouraging or unreliable information, so he's trying to offset the lies with some of God's truth about who you really are. Do your best to listen to him.

MEET YOUR DAD IN THE MIDDLE

Ask your dad to take you shopping. Let him give you a budget and establish a plan for what you are shopping for (summer clothes, a church dress, etc.). Explain to him what is in style and what your friends are wearing. Welcome his feedback on what looks nice, but it's okay if you have to teach him a few things about what works and what doesn't. Listen to what he might share about how guys view the "sexy" aspect of beauty. Don't pitch a fit if he has to "veto" certain outfits that he feels might not be appropriate.

SOME THINGS TO TALK ABOUT

*Tell your dad how you typically see yourself. Are you pretty? Are there times you compare yourself to others and feel you don't measure up?

*Do you notice other girls who get attention from friends or boys based on how they dress? Are you tempted to do that, as well?

*If your parents are married, ask what things your dad noticed in your mom? What part did external beauty have? How about her heart and mind? How has that "evolved" over time?

*Coach your dad on what he can do to encourage you in this area.

5

Guys

At some point, the heart of most every girl goes through a significant transformation. She realizes that the boys whom she recently thought of as gross and covered in cooties have somehow become quite tolerable. In fact, they even seem attractive. The very people who disgusted her just a few short years ago can quickly become the focus of much of her heart and mind.

If you haven't experienced this yet, it will come soon enough. God has probably put in your heart a longing to be pursued and desired by a young man. You likely dream of the perfect guy one day sweeping you off your feet. And even if you aren't thinking about "Mr. Wonderful" just yet, it is normal to simply desire to be the target of someone's affections. At some level, every girl wants to be loved and pursued.

Even at just a "friend level," guys are pretty awesome. With all the drama that can occur with your girl friends, the stability of a guy friend is a refreshing change. Movies often capture this platonic friendship well, though they often blossom into a romantic relationship within the two-hour story arc of a film. Doing that in real life (without someone getting hurt) can be a challenge.

The key for young women like you who aren't quite ready for marriage is learning to navigate your relationships with guys. This can be challenging, because young men and young women come from such radically different places it terms of maturity, emotional intelligence, and even in their motivation and capacity for having a romantic relationship.

WHY YOUR PERSPECTIVE OF GUYS MATTERS

Before your desire to enter a relationship with a guy gets cranked up to full blast, you need a plan for how to manage all the feelings you will likely experience. If you don't think about how and when and why you will date or get serious with a guy, you will likely just do whatever feels right at the time. You won't think about the implications and effects of what you are doing.

Much of what you hear from the world around you says to "follow your heart." You hear that message in the movies, in popular music, and in the very ethos of your generation. Believe it or not, you have been fed a steady diet of that type of drivel from the Disney princess movies you watched when you were younger. And it hasn't stopped. The message is relentless so it is what you probably know by default.

In contrast, Jeremiah 17:9 speaks about the questionable reliability of the heart: *"The heart is deceitful above all things and beyond cure. Who can understand it?"* According to Scripture, following one's heart can be synonymous with following a lie. It cannot be trusted and it is not always reasonable. However, because of your exposure to the "follow your heart" message, you may not know that there is a better way. It is possible to interact with guys with some measure of intention and purpose.

> ***"If you are looking for a guy to fill a void, he is going to let you down."***

Statistically speaking, you will likely one day be married. Your interactions with guys and eventually your romantic relationships with them have the potential to set the pace for your most important long-term relationship. What you do before marriage matters. How you see yourself (and how a guy fits into that) matters.

THE LIE YOU ARE LED TO BELIEVE

Plenty of girls you know work very hard to get guys to notice them. The way they dress or flirt guarantees some measure of attention. From your perspective, it can almost feel like a contest...one that you are probably losing. Other girls are getting ahead and you are falling behind. You may find yourself believing that your worth is rooted in who notices you or who likes you.

In spite of what feminism has told you about independence and self-sufficiency, you will still be tempted to think that you have value if a boy says you do. That's why many girls crave the attention of stupid, immature guys. It's also why they will compromise their values sexually to gain or maintain a guy's affections. (More on that in the next chapter.)

> *"Having a crush is not a bad thing. But if you're not ready for a relationship, you don't have to tell him. Better yet, don't tell anybody else."*

The desire to pair up and be "Facebook official" is a real thing. The net result is that you might feel the pressure to have a boyfriend long before you're ready. If some of your friends are in relationships, you can begin to believe the lie that they are blissfully connected while you are hopelessly alone.

The reality is that most relationships in middle and high school are just plain silly. Nobody grows. Nobody matures. It's a self-centered pursuit that is a far cry from the sacrificial love that will be required from you in marriage one day. Most teen romances result in wasted time and broken hearts. There has to be a better way!

THE ACTUAL TRUTH

As your heart begins to awaken to an interest in guys and a desire to know and be known intimately, you must constantly remember a few key truths. It might be a good idea to remind your girlfriends of these things, as well.

You need to know that you are valuable apart from a guy. You are loved by God and have worth whether a guy notices you or not. Marriage will likely be in your future, (God said in Genesis that it is not good for us to be alone) but the Bible does not make it prescriptive for every person. That means that no man will "complete" a woman. You need to know that.

You also need to remember that the typical teenage guy is immature and self-centered. Just as you have not yet learned to love selflessly, that cute guy you have taken an interest in probably has no comprehension at all of what true sacrificial love is. His interest in you is, at some level, motivated by a selfish need for personal or even sexual gratification. If you're honest, your desires for a guy's attention are pretty self-centered, as well.

"Be careful not to become addicted to the affirmation that guys give you."

Finally, you need to know that one of your father's jobs is to help you to navigate your relationships with guys. That means that it will sometimes feel like he is too curious about your romantic interests. He doesn't do this to be mean, but because he loves you.

The Song of Solomon contains some of the intimate words sung between lovers. It's sort of the "sexy" book in the Bible. On three different occasions the Scriptures say, *"Do not arouse or awaken love until it so desires."* (Song of Solomon 2:7, 3:5, and 8:4)

While Solomon's bride may have simply been telling her "little sisters" to let her man sleep late, I think there is a deeper meaning here. The entire book is devoted to describing the intense love and passion that is being experienced. It is like a wild beast that, once awakened, cannot be tamed.

In that context, the lovers are both describing the powerful force that they now know AND they are warning their younger siblings to not go there until they are absolutely ready to handle it. The experience is so powerful, intoxicating, and life-changing, they had better not unleash it until they are ready. Once it is awakened, it is difficult to turn off.

Regrettably, our culture encourages girls like you to awaken love as soon as possible, and as often as possible. The result is that you are forced to grapple with the complications and challenges of giving your fully-awakened heart away, only to see it trampled on by one jerk-faced guy after another who are mainly concerned with their own needs.

> *"You are not ready to have a relationship until you are mature enough. You probably aren't mature enough at 15."*

God will one day bring the right guy into your life when you and he are mature enough and ready to offer true selfless love to each other. Until that time, God's coaching to you is to keep your romantic heart in check until you are ready.

HOW YOU CAN BE DIFFERENT

1. Slow Down

Even if your friends are moving aggressively into relationships with guys, you don't have to. In fact, studies show that girls who enter and end a lot of relationships tend to have less satisfaction in marriage. Romantic relationships are one area where practice doesn't make perfect. It just makes you good at breaking up when things aren't going your way.

For now, think through your plan for dating. Can you go to a dance or on a date with a guy without it turning into a major relationship? Do you even need to be in a relationship? How will you know you are ready? These would be great things to talk about with your dad.

2. Look Carefully for the Right Attributes in Guys

One way to identify what you desire in a spouse is by simply observing the guys around you. For the guys in your life, what do you like about them? What would it be like to be married to someone like that someday? What about him might begin to annoy you after a while?"

A handsome and charming guy will always draw attention, but you can also learn to look a little closer at a guy by considering a few deeper issues of character:

*How does he treat others?

*Does he operate with humility?

*How does he spend his free time?

*How does he respond to authority?

*Does he speak naturally about his relationship with God?

That last question is vitally important because you want to be with a guy who is accountable to God for how he loves and treats you. If he's not, he will do whatever feels right to his fickle heart in the moment. A guy who has passion but no character to back it up is always going to be the wrong guy.

3. Focus on Becoming the Right Person

While the questions above can serve as a great filter to examine the guys in your world, they can also serve as a guide as you look in the mirror. In addition to looking for the right person, you should first and foremost work on *becoming* the right person. Andy Stanley says it this way: "Be the person the person you are looking for is looking for."

HOW YOUR DAD CAN HELP

As you begin to take an interest in guys, you should count on your dad for guidance. Trust his opinions and perspectives. Welcome his questions about your relationships.

> *"What the people around you think about your boyfriend is actually more valuable than what YOU think of him."*

This might seem like a pain at first, but you should also welcome any boundaries your dad gives on who and how and when you date. Nothing good will come of sneaking behind your parents' back to delve into a relationship with a guy. God gave your dad the job of watching out for you, so when you rebel against it, you are actually rebelling against God. That is never a smart thing to do.

One more thing related to that: There is a principle found in 2 Corinthians 6:14 about being *"equally-yoked."* This is God's reminder to not be in a relationship with someone who doesn't share your faith. That's why it's foolish to go on a single date (even as friends to a dance) with someone who wouldn't ultimately be a potential spouse. After all, it's possible to fall in love with anybody.

Finally, one great guideline to consider is that any boy who wants to date or enter a relationship with you has to talk to your dad first. This serves first and foremost as a simple way to weed out the losers. If a guy has an interest in you but refuses to have a simple conversation with your dad, then why would you waste your time on him? Trust us.... he's a bum.

In addition to that, you also want your dad to know the guy you are interested in. You will value his perspective on what the guy is like. Your dad will be able to offer a measure of accountability to the both of you as you enter this new relationship. It may sound weird, but you need this. More on this in chapter eight.

MEET YOUR DAD IN THE MIDDLE

Go on a dinner date with your dad and let him show you (by example) how you can expect to be treated by the boys who take you out. Talk about boundaries and expectations. Just as every man loves to be encouraged and affirmed, say some nice things about your dad, telling him what you love and value about him.

SOME THINGS TO TALK ABOUT

*Share with your dad some of the guys you have had a crush on through the years. Share what made you take an interest in those guys? Are they reasons of substance?

*Ask your dad about the hormonal drives of many teenage guys and what motivates them to be in a relationship. What was your dad like as a teenager?

*Ask your dad about what sorts of things he would look for if he were literally in charge of picking a spouse for you. Do you agree with his suggestions? Why or why not?

6

Sex

We need to talk about sex. Everybody else in our world is, so why shouldn't we? In addition, most of what you are hearing is bad information, so we need to set the record straight on a few important things.

First of all, let's make it clear that God invented sex. God is not freaked out by it. In fact, He wants every person He created – including you – to experience His amazing gift of sexuality. But as the designer of sex, He gets exclusive rights to define how it works. Sexual activity of any kind is best expressed only in a heterosexual, covenant marriage relationship.

But just like everything awesome that God has created for us to enjoy, His enemy is passionately devoted to screwing it up. What is supposed to be a wonderful and satisfying part of our lives is, for many people, the source of their greatest regret, pain and shame. Girls like you need to be committed to getting sex right, because there is such a high likelihood of getting it wrong.

This is potentially awkward territory, but our desire here is to tee up some meaningful conversations about sexuality with your dad. Just because something is cringe-worthy, that doesn't mean that it's not important. While your mom might take the lead in talking to you about how babies are made or your monthly cycle, there are some topics where your dad's words and influence are incredibly valuable. As a man, he has a unique perspective of how most guys view sex. Odd as it might seem, he might actually have something meaningful to contribute.

WHY YOUR VIEW OF SEX MATTERS

First, here's a little bad news about your brain. Because it is still developing, you are less able to consider the long-term consequences of your decisions. The result is that you tend to focus on the here and now. This is huge as it relates to sexual activity.

"When it comes to the long-term impact of your sexual behavior, you have no idea what you are dealing with."

What you do sexually before marriage has significant power to negatively impact your future marriage relationship. This is something that few people in our culture will tell you. Studies have shown that the more you connect physically with guys who are not you husband, the greater the likelihood that your marriage will not make it.

South African pastor P.J. Smyth captures it this way:

"When I lived in Harare, Zimbabwe, close to our flat was the most enormous hole in the ground about the size of half a football field, and at least 40 meters deep. It was the foundation for a huge skyscraper. The bizarre thing was that during the pause in the work between digging the hole and starting to build, the site was totally unguarded for a few weeks. If I had the desire, I could have got down into the bottom of the hole without much difficulty. Why were there no guards? Because there was nothing to protect, of course!

But let's imagine that for some reason I wanted to destroy the building. Rather than take a wrecking ball to it once it was up, I would be cunning to sneak down into the unguarded foundation, dig a couple of grave-size holes, lay some explosives that I set on a three year fuse, cover it over, climb out, walk away and relax for three years! And the beauty of it would be that they would probably never suspect that it was me!

The foundation of your marriage is your pre-marriage years. If Satan can sneak in and mess you up during those foundational years, then he is well on the way to destroying your marriage in the future."

As counselors, we see the effects of this "pre-marriage time bomb" in the marriages we see struggling today, but the problems are compounded for your generation. You are growing up in a culture that is more sexualized, encourages more casual relationships, and is loading you up with more emotional baggage than your parents' generation ever dreamed of.

THE LIE YOU ARE LED TO BELIEVE

Your culture suggests that sex should be free of boundaries, focused on self, and a reasonable part of any romantic relationship. If you don't embrace an alternative message, you are likely to buy what the world is selling, even if it's a horrible counterfeit to God's design.

"Movies and music are telling you a bunch of really wrong stuff."

The music, TV, and movies you see affirm the normalcy of emotionally and physically significant relationships, even in high school. Your regular diet of this content tends to foster a perspective that such relationships are both expected and necessary.

At 16, when you and your friends start to drive, things can escalate quickly. Freed from the restrictions of parents and the limitations of group activities, couples will likely see intimate kissing, sexual touching, oral sex, and even intercourse as normal, reasonable dimensions of their relationship. While you might think, "I would never do that," it happens quicker than you would ever imagine. Emotional intimacy can easily transition to sexual intimacy in any romantic relationship.

THE ACTUAL TRUTH

This moment calls for a chemistry lesson. Specifically, you

need to know about a powerful little chemical called oxytocin. This "drug" has the potential to influence you more than alcohol, marijuana, and all other illegal substances combined. It will give you a better understanding of why you need to guard your sexuality so carefully.

Oxytocin is known in scientific circles as "the bonding chemical." It is secreted in both men and women, helping to create meaningful bonds and attachments to others. It also gives one a sense of euphoria in the deepest places of our mind and body. As you might expect, oxytocin is most powerfully generated in times of sexual intimacy. Unfortunately, oxytocin doesn't have a brain. It doesn't know if you are connecting to someone worth connecting to. Oxytocin is one of the reasons that sex literally makes people stupid.

Sexual activity outside of marriage has the potential to make you stay bonded with a complete bozo. It's why two young people who seem to have nothing in common and who are rarely seen getting along very well can't seem to break up. They are confusing lust with love and oxytocin is effectively serving as the fuel that's powering their stupidity. To be blunt, sexual intimacy masks relationship flaws.

The good news is that God created oxytocin to work in marriage. It generates powerful bonds and keeps two people crazy in love with one another. It does just the opposite in teen relationships. It might keep a couple coming back to one another, but it undermines the substantive parts of the relationship that are necessary to last long-term.

Even in the Bible's original language, God made an important distinction between sex before marriage and sex in marriage. The English language has one main word for sex: it's sex. That word is used to describe a great big variety of behaviors and activities.

But in the original Hebrew of the Bible, God was careful to show us extreme contrasts in the different types of sex. One word for sex, *yada*, is used to describe sex within marriage. It's the word used to describe the perfect and secure intimacy that Adam and Eve experienced: *"Now Adam had sexual relations with his wife, Eve, and she became pregnant."* (Genesis 4:1) The word for sex here implies *"to know."* It is an extreme level of intimacy reserved for marriage.

In contrast, there are plenty of places in the biblical narrative where God is describing the sexual act, but it's not happening in marriage. In many of those instances, the Bible will usually use the word *shakab*. It implies more of a *"spilling of seed."* It is a meaningless physical act, not rooted in anything of substance.

Dannah Gresh puts it this way: "Some sex is God's sex. It's *yada*. Some sex is a mere counterfeit. It's *shakab*. Same plumbing, but a total different thing." Be assured, if you're messing around with a guy, you may feel close to him, but it's still *shakab*.

> *"If you have to do something physical to get a guy to stay, he is without a doubt the wrong guy."*

God wants us to deny ourselves the shallow, selfish experience of *shakab* so we can best experience the intimate knowing found in *yada*. He wants us to fully enjoy

His gift of sex, free of all the baggage that most people pick up as they navigate their teen and young adult years. That's why He tells us to wait.

HOW YOU CAN BE DIFFERENT

1. Set Some Personal Boundaries

Making a decision about saving sex for marriage is one thing. Following through with that commitment is another. It is especially hard when you don't know where to draw the line. Sure, sexual intercourse is for marriage, but what about everything else?

Maybe you're asking the wrong question. Don't ask, "How far is too far?" That's like saying, "How close can I get to sinning without actually sinning?" Instead, ask, "How can I best honor God with my sexuality?" He might call you to radical purity, something that few of your friends are committed to, but it will be worth it.

> *"Culture has twisted our definition of sex so much. Don't believe the hype."*

2. Believe that your Sexuality is Worth Guarding

There are two reasons you often hear for saving sex for marriage: pregnancy and sexually transmitted diseases. But those are not the best reasons to wait. You need a bigger, grander reason to not settle for anything but God's very best.

Something as beautiful and holy and fulfilling as "*yada*" shouldn't be treated casually like "*shakab*." Your God-given sexuality is a precious thing that has incredible potential to create joy and bring intimacy to your marriage. It is worth protecting, so try not to be careless with your sexuality.

"Drugs and alcohol can cause you to forget your principles and do stupid stuff. They cause you do let your guard down. That's why you have to stay sober."

3. Know that God is All About Forgiveness

While we need to stress that it is better to save sexual activity for marriage, we also know that many people blow it. They compromise their values and do things they later regret. If that's you, don't beat yourself up over it. You are not damaged goods.

The central message of the gospel is that Jesus offers His grace when we fall short of His standards. We never measure up and He loves us anyway. When you fail, Satan will be there to tell you the lie that God doesn't want you anymore. That could not be any further from the truth. God loves us in spite of our sins, even if we fail over and over again. Keep running back to Him. Receive His forgiveness and then seek His help to get it right next time.

"If you mess up, there's always a second chance."

HOW YOUR DAD CAN HELP

As the man whom God has given the responsibility of raising you, your dad is uniquely placed to help you make wise choices regarding your sexuality. Sure, it might feel like he's something of a watchdog for your romantic life, but that's one of his jobs. If you let him do it (and he is tender and tactful), you will probably look back and be thankful that he was something of a nuisance regarding this area of your teen years.

Your dad might also help you to come up with some "scripts" to get out of any uncomfortable situations you encounter with guys. In other words, you need to talk about "fleeing sexual temptation" long before your prom date. Too many girls are ill prepared for what they eventually face because no one has helped them to get ready. Let your dad help with this.

MEET YOUR DAD IN THE MIDDLE

Sometime when you are riding in the car together, be courageous enough to let your dad know that talking about sexual issues with him is incredibly awkward. (In the car is best because you are shoulder-to-shoulder and you don't have to look each other in the eye.) Tell him that you need his help but not his judgment. If you feel judged, you are less likely to share anything with him. Give him permission to speak into your life if he ever senses that you are letting your guard down regarding your sexuality.

SOME THINGS TO TALK ABOUT

*Back in your dad's day, parents tried to keep sexual content from their kids. Today, it's more like kids are trying to keep sexual content from their parents. Is that true today? Why or why not?

*Discuss the implications of oxytocin mentioned above. Why does it matter?

*Talk about what parameters might be wise for your dad to set up to keep you from stepping outside of God's boundaries regarding sex.

7

Pornography

It's easy to see porn as simply a "guy" issue. But with the easy-accessibility (and privacy) of internet porn, more and more young women are becoming users. That means more and more curious teenage girls are looking. And they are getting hooked.

Porn affects everybody, including girls. We see this more and more frequently in the stories of the young newlywed girls we mentor who tell us that they have been hooked on porn since their college years. And most recently, we have heard it in the testimony of a young woman our family knows well.

Nicole was raised right. She has terrific parents. She was homeschooled for most of her life and was involved in a great church. And she struggled with porn. None of us are off-limits to a crafty enemy who wants to derail our spiritual and sexual lives. The minute you let your guard down and declare, "It will never happen to me," is the moment you are vulnerable.)

After several years of porn entanglement, Nicole has seen God do a fresh work of restoration in her heart. While she may struggle with the temptation all her life, she is now walking in victory. She has even shared her story on her blog, encouraging countless other young women who have struggled as she did. I only wish that redemption and joy were at the end of every life's story that has been impacted by porn. Tragically, it is not.

WHY GUARDING YOUR EYES MATTERS

Dr. Chap Clark of the Fuller Youth Institute says that 60% of teen boys in America are addicted to porn. He defined "addicted" as 3 visits per week to a porn site at one hour per visit. The statistics on porn use among teenage girls are almost as bad. One study determined that more than a third of teenage girls reported that they had watched porn recently.

"Girls have the potential to struggle too! Don't you get it?! The Lord didn't create sex for men only!"

This early exposure to graphic sexual content has the real potential to become a full-fledged addiction. Because habitual porn use gives a dopamine rush, brain pathways are established and new patterns of behavior are fostered. Scientists say that it is just as significant and powerful as any drug addiction. Porn use can literally re-shape your brain.

Online pornography is also giving an entire generation a

lousy education about sex. The work we have done with young newlywed couples has convinced us that there is some bad news for the smartphone generation. Too many young couples have a terrible perspective about what sex is and what God meant for it to be. As is common with many guys, a girl's porn habit now will likely be carried into marriage. Rarely does the addiction simply "go away" once they walk down the aisle.

The bottom line is that potential for private, sexual sin is very high for girls today. If you are not diligent to guard your eyes, the chances of stumbling into it (and then staying) are incredibly high.

THE LIE YOU ARE LED TO BELIEVE

To look at porn, your grandfather's generation had to head to a seedy adult theater in a bad part of town. Thanks to Hugh Hefner, the creator of Playboy magazine, your dad's generation experienced a shift in the "normalization" of explicit content. Even still, up to about 25 years ago, people had to get porn from a public place, like an adult bookstore.

Fast forward to today. Exposure to (and the use of) porn has become the more normalized in your culture and among your friends. The reasoning goes that if something can be easily accessed via a smartphone or a home computer, then it must be okay. As I heard one teenager recently say, "Everyone looks at it, so it must not be a big deal."

Unfortunately, all this early exposure to porn is impacting how teenagers discover and experiment with their own sexuality. What boys expect from girls has changed, with oral sex becoming, in some circles, as common as "making out." In her groundbreaking book, "Girls and Sex," author Peggy Orenstein shares how many young women feel obligated to gratify the sexual requests of guys who have come to see porn as the standard for sexual behavior.

In the broad sense, porn in our culture has de-sensitized us all to sexual content. We're no longer shocked by it anymore. What God meant to be private and holy and beautiful has become a casual thing. You have to be entirely unconventional (and something of a weirdo) to believe that a person's sexuality is still precious and worth protecting.

THE ACTUAL TRUTH

An entire generation is learning about sex from looking at online pornography, and they are getting a terrible education. Simply put, watching porn to learn about sex is sort of like playing Nintendo Mario Cart to learn how to drive. It's just not helpful.

"Porn is not real. It gives a horrible view of sex."

While porn is an easy source for (bad) sex education, there is a far better source to get your questions answered. The book your dad is reading encourages him and your mom to be available to you as reliable sources of information about sex. Even though it is uncomfortable, you need to talk about this stuff with someone who is looking out for you and who will tell you the truth. Obviously, your mom is the first place to start, but there are some topics that your dad can help with. The porn conversation is one of those.

For now, know that the entire dynamic of sex displayed in the typical porn video is a lie. Sex in porn is usually guy-focused and the girl is just a tool to meet his desires. If you believe that (or the guy you date believes that) you are missing out on the fundamental role that sex has in the marriage relationship. It's about oneness, intimacy, AND pleasure. It's not about getting what you want but about generously giving to your spouse. Sex in porn undermines all of that. That's why it is so critical that you avoid it.

Long before the modern pornography industry introduced the possibility of sexual sin that can be experienced in private, God knew it would be a reality. Whether it's our thought life or the deliberate seeking out of explicit images and videos, we are all prone to foolish sexual behavior. Given how easy it is to struggle with this, God gives a very simple prescription for any girl who doesn't want porn to distort or undermine her sex life.

In I Corinthians 6:18, the Bible gives us a strong warning about sexual sin. It says, *"Flee from sexual immorality. All other sins a person commits are outside the body, but whoever sins sexually, sins against their own body."* This word speaks to both the seriousness of sexual sin and the simple (though not always easy) solution.

> *"Just because it's not on a porn site, doesn't mean it's not porn. Check your heart and motivation with everything you let your eyes see."*

Here's a practical application of God's standard: If you ever encounter even a hint of sexually explicit content, you need to flee. Run. Get out of there. Remove yourself immediately from the situation. The longer you flirt with it, the harder it will be to disengage from it.

This is important because no other behavior operates quite like a "slippery slope" more than sexual sin. The more porn you see, the more you want to look. Typically, the content becomes more and more explicit as you go deeper down the rabbit hole. While some things might seem harmless, they have the high likelihood of leading to more destructive – and habit forming – content. That's why the best solution is to flee.

HOW YOU CAN BE DIFFERENT

Talking about fleeing sexual sin and actually doing it are entirely different things. That's why you need to develop some skills and principles related to how you will respond to our "pornified" culture.

1. Learn to Bounce Your Eyes

A simple skill that every person needs to learn is the "eye bounce." Sure, we will notice sexual images all around us, but we can choose to immediately look away. First mentioned in his book "Every Man's Battle," Stephen Arterburn suggests that a lot can happen in that split-second when we first notice an image that is sexual in nature. Before a look or a thought takes hold in our minds, we can quickly move on to something else. It's like a quick conversation with yourself that says, "That's not for me."

"Curiosity can be dangerous. Even if you are just looking at other girls, it has the power to stir the wrong stuff within you."

It's sort of like the truth that Job declared in Job 31:1. His commitment was simple: *"I made a covenant with my eyes not to look lustfully at a young woman."* If this faithful man had to make a commitment to protect his eyes, then every one of us would be wise to do likewise. Strive to be diligent in this, asking God's help to do in you what you are likely unable to easily do on your own.

2. Assume the Boys You Know are Looking at Porn

Not every guy is looking at porn every day, but studies show that the vast majority of them are at least struggling with it. Consider this not as a reason to judge them, but for two other, more important reasons. First, you need to have compassion on the young men in your life. Pray for their purity and their holiness.

Second, consider how common porn use is for guys as you enter romantic relationships with them. Their porn habit might impact how they treat you or what they expect from you. If a guy's sexual expectations have been distorted because of what he has seen through the years, you may need to distance yourself relationally from him until he can repent from his sin and reboot his brain. Don't ever compromise your principles because of a guy's sexual advances.

3. Value Parameters on Your Technology

According to parenting expert Rob Rienow, "Nobody is holy enough to have a private online life." There is value in having accountability or filtering software on every device that you use. Knowing that someone is occasionally looking over your shoulder to see what you are doing online provides a great sense of comfort. This simple safeguard might keep you from walking down a path that is not easy to get off of.

"Once you start looking, it can be very hard to stop."

Because most filters have flaws, you're going to have to learn to govern yourself. God can help with this. So can your parents. Be willing to have occasional conversations with them about why porn is dangerous and then do whatever you have to do to stay far from it.

HOW YOUR DAD CAN HELP

Gladly submitting to any filtering and accountability plans he might offer is a great way that you can let your dad lead you. Beyond that, your dad might have insights you can use. Because porn has historically been more of a guy problem than a girl problem, he probably understands better than anyone you know just how real the struggle is. Allow him to share how he or his friends dealt with porn back when he was young, but also ask him to share about how real his struggle is even today.

Your dad can talk to you about the way that porn use might affect the brains and hearts of the guys that you will date. When the time comes for you to enter a serious dating relationship, encourage him to hold your boyfriend accountable to making wise choices regarding what he sees online. Like many of these conversations, it might be awkward, but it is so important.

Finally, if like in Nicole's story, you are already struggling with a desire to look at porn, you need to get some help. It starts with telling someone you trust. Your parents can walk through this with you, helping you to turn from your sin and to start walking free. It's God's plan for you to get this right, but you can't do it alone.

MEET YOUR DAD IN THE MIDDLE

Talk with your dad about the reality of sexually explicit content and discuss the need for accountability and safeguards in your home. Do some research together on some of the filtering and accountability tools available on the market today and then decide on one that will work for your family. (We recommend tools such as Circle and Covenant Eyes.) Also, ask your dad if you can have a role in holding him accountable to sexual purity in a world of porn. Agree that this is a struggle for every person in your family and that you are committed to helping each other to walk in victory.

SOME THINGS TO TALK ABOUT

*Discuss how porn use might negatively affect the guys you will date. If someone has looked at porn, does that rule him out as a possible spouse? Why or why not?

*Talk a whole lot about the grace of God for our sin.... particularly the sexual sin that gives so many people shame. Discuss how the grace of God forgives us completely.

8

Security

Over the past year, story after story has surfaced of women who have been taken advantage of by men in positions of power. Starting with movie producer Harvey Weinstein, hundreds of men have been brought in to account for their past sexual aggressions and abuses. This is a very good thing. It's as if our entire culture has finally declared that we are not going to tolerate men behaving badly.

This sort behavior is more common than most of us could ever imagine. It doesn't just happen in Hollywood. Perhaps you have seen #MeToo or #NoMore written by someone you know and love. These simple hash tags are giving a voice to the millions of women (and men) who have experienced some form of unwanted sexual activity. People are now talking openly about horrible incidents that they had previously kept secret. We are learning that many of our friends have experienced some form of abuse.

The reality is that there will always be men who will take advantage of women. Most guys are well intentioned, but somewhere along the way, you will likely interact with some who are not. In the workplace, at a party, or even on a date, you might one day be shocked at how that super-nice guy isn't so nice after all.

In the case that you encounter a #MeToo situation in your own life, God wants to prepare you to protect yourself. Your dad can help with this. From his perspective, you were easy to protect when you were a little girl and safely at home. But you're in the process of growing up and moving on. That's why you need to let him prepare you for what might happen in the world out there.

WHY YOUR DAD'S PROTECTION MATTERS

Most girls like you have been blessed to live in somewhat of an insulated bubble. Your parents have probably protected you from a lot of the ugly things that happen in our world. Unfortunately, that means you might be a bit oblivious as to just how common physical and sexual abuse is. You might not be on guard because you don't realize that it happens so much.

The statistics are hard to quantify (because so much abuse goes unreported), but more than 80% of women have experienced some form of sexual harassment. One study suggests that one out of every three women will be a victim of either sexual assault or domestic violence at some point in their lives. We can hope that what has been brought to light in recent days via #MeToo is changing that. No longer are victims of abuse shamed into silence, afraid of the repercussions of disclosure.

While we have all heard the stories of assault in the workplace that make headlines, there are also the potentially aggressive actions of the young men that you will date. Unfortunately, being alone with a guy who has less-than-noble intentions can lead to a situation with significant emotional (and even physical) casualties.

"You assume that cute guy is a gentleman...until he isn't. In the wrong circumstances, sexual aggression can happen fast."

It would be great to be able to give every man the benefit of the doubt. Most men don't have evil intentions. But as long as men are stronger than women (and boys are stronger than girls), there will always be some risk of you being taken advantage of. That is why you have to be prepared. Helping you stay safe and protected is one of the jobs that God has given your father.

THE LIE YOU ARE LED TO BELIEVE

There was a huge sexual revolution in the 60's and 70's. It was perhaps the biggest shift in history where sex outside of marriage –free love, they called it – was celebrated among young people. With your generation's easy access to porn via today's technology, we are seeing a different sort of sexual revolution.

Girls from your generation have been given a mixed message regarding their sexuality. You are told that you should be just as sexual as guys can be. This is supposed to be empowering. But while women can certainly be just as sexual as men, I don't think the sexual empowerment message has done young women any favors, especially in light of the "pornification" of many men.

"I can't believe how much porn has effected the sexual expectations of the guys I date. It's so messed up!"

Think about it. An entire generation of young men is learning (through porn) that girls want sex without any commitment or emotional connection.

On the other hand, our culture has demonized any man who treats a woman as a toy to be played with. We should not be surprised when men like Harvey Weinstein act badly. Or when an 18-year-old guy aggressively pursues sexual favors from the girl he is dating. It's a confusing mess.

The net result is that young women like you are left vulnerable. This may be the sad reality of our world, but you don't have to like it. Or even tolerate it. You can strive to be prepared and on guard.

THE ACTUAL TRUTH

As you grow up and gain more freedom in your world, you need to know that your dad is there to protect you. While he might not always be present with you, he can prepare you for what you will face. And if something ever happens where you feel vulnerable, he can be the person you run to for help and rescue. No matter how old you are, this is his job until you marry and he passes that responsibility over to your husband.

One of the worst things about the breakdown in the father/daughter relationship is that girls don't feel safe going to their fathers for help. They are embarrassed, or they feel that dad won't understand what they are going through. The result is that girls are left to fend for themselves when God has given them an advocate and protector in their fathers.

You need to know that your dad is there for you, even if he seems a bit clueless at times. Remember, there are no manuals on raising daughters. Just like you, he is figuring this out as he goes along. He may come off as unsure, but don't mistake that for disinterest. He cares for you more than you know, even if he doesn't know how to show it. The last thing he wants is for you to feel alone and unprotected on his watch.

"There are things I kept from my dad that, looking back now, I know I should have shared with him."

Because he is not always going to be present with you, you're going to have to learn some skills to protect yourself. A part of that is learning to steer clear of circumstances where you might be vulnerable. Specifically, you need to learn how to look for "red flags" in potentially risky situations. There's a great example of this in God's word.

1 Samuel 13 tells the tragic story of David's son Amnon and his sick obsession with his sister Tamar. It serves as a cautionary tale and a textbook case of someone who missed all the warning signs. Amnon desperately wanted to have sex with Tamar, so at the suggestion of one of his advisors, he devised a plan to get her alone. He pretended to be sick and then asked his father David to send Tamar to care for him and make him some homemade bread. Grab a Bible

and take a minute to read the entire story.

The first person to miss a red flag was David, Tamar's father. Whether he was too busy to notice Amnon's obsession or he was simply naïve, we do not know. What we do know is that David sent his daughter into a very hazardous situation.

Tamar went to Amnon's room and made bread right there in his presence. She did just as he requested, but Amnon wouldn't eat it. He suddenly acted like he wasn't interested. There's the second red flag. He said one thing and did another. If a guy ever changes his plans about where he is taking you or what his plans are, you know it's time to put your guard up.

The third red flag that Tamar should have noticed was when Amnon sent everyone else out of his room, leaving her alone with him. This is clearly significant. A good rule to live by is to avoid being alone in any isolated place with a guy, even if he has proven himself trustworthy. You and he may have the best of intentions, but the potential for temptation is just too great when no one else is around.

A final red flag came when Amnon asked Tamar to sit on his bed and feed him. This was the same guy who just a few minutes ago said he wasn't hungry. In those moments when you sense that something isn't right, it is probably because something isn't right. That troubling sense is most likely the Holy Spirit of God warning you to flee.

In Tamar's case, she could have seen some of the red flags, expressed a measure of discomfort with the whole situation, and bolted for the door. Because she didn't, she suffered a sexual assault at the hands of someone she trusted.

HOW YOU CAN BE DIFFERENT

1. Be Empowered and Believe You are Strong

You need to know that you have a voice and that you can use it. If you don't like something or if you ever feel uncomfortable in a situation, you are allowed to say so. There is power in your voice and no one can take that power away from you. No matter the situation, you can always say "NO" or "STOP" if you feel uncomfortable with a guy. You can always report a boss or coworker if you feel they are abusing their position of authority in your life.

> *"Back when I was 15, I wish I had more confidence in myself. I wish I knew then that I didn't have to take crap from anybody; especially a guy."*

It begins with you getting comfortable with the tools of preparation, clear personal boundaries, and personal power. There are a lifetime of these lessons to learn, often practiced in the most risky of situations. Ultimately, it starts with you knowing that you never have to settle for being passive. You don't ever have to go along with anything when you are the least bit uncomfortable.

2. Strive to Be a "Hard Target"

If you watch a television show about African wildlife on a nature channel, you probably get a quick lesson about predators and prey. A hungry lion will always pick out the most weak and frail animal from within a herd for his lunch. A guy looking to take advantage of a girl will do the same.

Be certain that using recreational drugs and alcohol can make you the target of sexual aggression. A few headline-grabbing trials in recent days have showed us that foolish and energetic young men have the real potential to take advantage of young women who are not fully sober. That's why drinking in social situations can be so dangerous.

You should also be aware that "date rape" drugs are a real thing. While the most popular one is Rohypnol (Roofies), other drugs commonly used include GHB, Ketamine, and even Ambien. It is not unheard of for charming and good-looking young men to slip them into girls' drinks at parties. A specific rule to live by: "At a party, do not EVER take a drink that someone gives you. Ever."

At parties or social situations when you are not sure of your environment, make it a personal policy to watch out for your girlfriends and make sure that your girlfriends are watching out for you.

HOW YOUR DAD CAN HELP

When you start falling for a guy, your emotions tend to cloud your judgment. It could be that the guy you like is awesome in every way, but your perspective of him might not be the only one to consider. You may need some "fresh eyes" to see the things that your smitten heart doesn't notice.

As your dad watches you interact with your guy, he may see some signs that you don't pick up on quite as easily. If he gives you advice or puts some parameters on your relationship, don't see it as a threat. Just trust that he is looking out for you, striving to offer the protection for you that God has given him the responsibility of offering.

MEET YOUR DAD IN THE MIDDLE

Scan the internet for news stories about men taking advantage of women. There are plenty of them to browse through. While an assault is never EVER the woman's fault, talk about ways that the women might have made themselves vulnerable or an easy target. Let your dad coach you on some specific personal boundaries that you might choose to enforce for yourself on dates and even in the workplace in order to stay safe.

SOME THINGS TO TALK ABOUT

*Ask you dad about what aggressive, hormonally charged guys might be capable of. When he was young and dumb, what was he capable of on his worst days?

*Talk about the importance of staying sober and alert.... and of watching out for your friends who might not be.

*Discuss how it might be awkward to confess to your dad that someone hurt you, but that your relationship needs to be safe enough that you can tell him anything.

9

God

As we write these words today, we are celebrating a big milestone in our second daughter's life. She got married this week in a private ceremony in a beautiful outdoor setting in California. We still can't believe that she is all grown up. These 22 years blazed by so incredibly fast!

Before you know it, the day will come when you will leave home and begin to live life on your own. No longer will your parents be there to lead you or to tell you what to do or when to be home. It will all be up to you. How will you ever function without them? It all depends.

How you do as an independent adult will hinge on at least a few things. Have your parents prepared you for the challenges you will face? Have they equipped you to manage friendships and romantic relationships with maturity? Have they given you confidence in yourself and the educational and real world opportunities to succeed in the path you have chosen? Have they instilled in you the character you will need to make wise choices in life?

All of these things matter, but one thing matters more than all of them combined. Specifically, you need to know God in a real and personal way. Not just know about God, but know Him personally.

You might be highly successful in every area of your life, but if you aren't connected to God, none of it ultimately matters. You need the direction, purpose, and peace that can only come through staying connected to your Creator.

"Making life decisions in submission to God gives me peace like nothing I have ever known."

Jesus made this very point to sisters Mary and Martha in Luke 10:38-42. Martha was busy with all sorts of household tasks while Mary was sitting at the feet of Jesus. Martha was ticked off, but Jesus told her, *"You are worried and upset about many things, but few things are needed— or indeed only one."* Jesus said that the one thing that matters is being close to Him. That's the most important life lesson you can ever learn.

WHY YOUR RELATIONSHIP WITH GOD MATTERS

Someone once said that the faith of the average 17-year-old is sort of like her 6th grade science fair project: mom and dad did all the work and she just put her name on it. I think that can be true. Counting on your parents' faith to carry you through life doesn't work, especially if you're not living under their roof. That is why it is essential that you learn now how to walk with God yourself.

God has always been there, wanting to lead and guide you towards an awesome and meaningful life. It's just that, during the teen years, it is very easy to allow your parents to take the place of God in your life. Why listen for the voice of God when you are required to listen to mom and dad?

> *"I came to Jesus in my late teens. Knowing now that God is in control of my life (and I am not) has changed everything for me. I wish I had known that when I was younger."*

Once you leave home, you will need God's guidance more than ever before. And in a world where some studies suggest that more than half of all Christian young people abandon their faith in college, the stakes have never been higher. You are going to encounter a world full of people who don't believe what you were likely raised to believe. How will your faith stand if it's not rooted in a solid relationship with Jesus?

THE LIE YOU ARE LED TO BELIEVE

Over the past few years, strange shifts have happened on the American college campus. Where you used to find great diversity of thought and generous freedom to debate varying worldviews, now you find more close-mindedness than ever before. Any diversion from the accepted politically correct viewpoint can be seen as hate-speech. In many environments, biblical Christianity is hate-speech.

As a result, many from your generation are landing at one

of three places regarding the place that God will play in their lives:

The first one concludes that God is irrelevant. It assumes that He is old-fashioned and no longer has a meaningful place in modern society. Given what we know about people and science and love, it is apparent that the way of life found in the Bible no longer has a place. Jesus was a nice guy and He taught some good things, but we can only rely on the parts that make us feel good about ourselves. It is entirely reasonable not to believe in God.

The second conclusion is that God is just one part of the American dream. You see this world-view embraced by many well-intentioned people in the Bible belt. You will likely encounter this view in many of your Christian friends on the college campus. They are nice people that will follow Jesus as long as following Jesus means a good career, a successful husband, two kids, and a nice house in a trendy part of town.

A final conclusion is that God is far away and doesn't need to be disturbed. These people believe that God is very busy. They might seek Him out when they are facing a big decision, but still choose to keep Him at arm's length in daily life. They miss out on the very relationship of love and intimacy that God has invited us into through Jesus.

THE ACTUAL TRUTH

Perhaps the most important truth you can know is that God is living, active, and relevant to you today. He has a plan for your life and is offering you the invitation to join Him in the big story of redemption He is telling in the world. While that starts when you submit to God's plan of salvation through faith in Jesus, it doesn't stop there. Through every part of your journey, you need to know that God is with you to lead you and guide you and give you an incredible life.

Even in those times when you get it wrong, God is there for you, offering His love and grace. He doesn't freak out when you sin, or fail, or choose the wrong path. While the enemy of our God might trick you into thinking that God is losing patience with you, He never ever does. He is constantly pursuing you, wanting to be close to you. There is nothing you can do to make God love you any more or any less. When you blow it, you can always run to Him.

> *"You're going to have bad days. Knowing that*
> *God is with you helps you to get through them."*

When seeking direction for life, or when confronted with temptation, God is there to lead you. Spending time talking with Jesus and feeding on scripture will put you in a position to know His will and to hear His voice. It has been said that those who know God's Word best hear His voice the clearest. Whoever said that was exactly right.

Charles Spurgeon once said, "Whatever is prominent in the Word of God should be conspicuous in our lives." God's word is full of examples of God speaking to His people through the relationship that He shared with them. This should be true of us, as well. In John 10:27, Jesus said, *"My sheep listen to my voice; I know them, and they follow me."*

While God will speak to you most clearly through His Word, He also has given you His Holy Spirit. That's His very presence that is with you everywhere you go. And make no mistake: God has a voice. He wants to speak to you. He wants to tell you who you are and what to do.

You might not hear some loud booming voice coming to you from the clouds, but God's Spirit can quietly whisper to your heart and mind in ways that you know that it's Him talking. Does that sound strange? It shouldn't. That's what He consistently did in the Bible.

Think about all the people in the Bible who heard God's voice in some way:

Adam, Noah, Abraham, Joseph, Moses, Joshua, Gideon, the Old Testament Prophets, Peter, Paul, John, etc. The list goes on and on.

It was normal in the Bible for the people of God to hear the voice of God. Why would we think that when the Bible narrative ended that somehow God stopped talking to the people He loves and wants to lead? That makes no sense. In fact, it's ludicrous to consider a "relationship with God" without two-way communication.

The key to staying close to God and hearing His voice is the simple act of being in love with Jesus. When you are in a love relationship with someone, you are motivated to be with them. The same holds true for God. You know how He has loved you and what He has done for you, so you respond with love. You want to know and talk to Him and to hear from Him.

> *"If you claim to be a Christian, then you have declared that Christ is your #1 priority in life. Take it seriously."*

Unfortunately, so many of us follow God out of obligation

or duty. Or maybe it's because our parents require it of us. It certainly isn't a result of our devoted love for Him. If that's the case in your life, you are missing out on the essential reality of the Christian life.

In addition to knowing what God is like, make it your priority to actually know Him. He's relational. Interact with Him. Talk to Him and listen to what He is trying to tell you.

HOW YOU CAN BE DIFFERENT

1. If You Haven't Already, Start a Relationship with God

We can talk about *being* in a relationship with God, but you have to start by *entering* a relationship with God. It doesn't happen automatically. God speaks to His followers, so you have to choose to be His follower.

Because He is completely holy and you are completely sinful, you have to come to God on His terms. That includes admitting that you are a sinner, trusting that Jesus paid the price for your sin on the cross, and committing yourself to Him as the new boss of your life. If you aren't clear on what it means to do that, ask someone you know who is fully committed to Jesus. You can be sure that they would be happy to lead you into a personal relationship with God.

2. Surround Yourself with Friends Who Know God

If you're going to stay close to Jesus, it is best done in the context of community. Identify those friends who share your desire to make your faith a priority. Then make it an intentional part of your time together to share what God is doing in your lives. Pray for and encourage each other to seek out God's very best.

You'll probably discover that there are a lot of people who go to church, but few who have fully committed their lives to Jesus. When you find these friends, stay close to them. They will be a treasure to you as you move through your life.

3. Cut Out Some Noise so You Can Hear God's Voice

It's hard to interact with a God you can't see when there are so many things fighting for your attention. You're probably a lot like those dogs in Pixar's *Up* movie. (Squirrel!!) You're easily distracted, so you may need to de-clutter your life. Turn off the TV, turn off the music, and fight the temptation to look at your smartphone whenever you have 60 seconds of free time.

Find some time every day that you can be still and quiet and connected with God. Talk to Him and be quiet long enough to let Him talk to you. And remember, God's voice will always match His Word. If you feel like God is telling you something that contradicts what you read in the Bible, you can be sure that it's not Him. But if it aligns with the Word and character of God, then it's probably His voice that you're hearing.

HOW YOUR DAD CAN HELP

Your dad is an imperfect guy, but maybe you can learn from him what it means to walk in a relationship with God.

If he is a Christ-follower, he can probably reflect on seasons of his life when he felt really close to God. Let him tell you about that.

As you get older and get closer to moving out on your own, your dad should be more and more focused on helping you to walk with God on your own. If he asks you about your relationship with God or what God is teaching you, see those as good questions. He's wanting you to "*taste and see that the Lord is good*" while he still has some influence in your life.

MEET YOUR DAD IN THE MIDDLE

Get your dad to tell you about some of the times in his life when he felt really close to God. Ask him what he was doing to draw close to God and what the result was in his daily life. To contrast that, ask him to share about some seasons of life when he was far from God. Ask him what distracted him from making God a priority and what life was like during that season. Talk about why walking with God is so important.

SOME THINGS TO TALK ABOUT

*Growing up in your home, do you feel like you have learned how to walk in a relationship with God or just gained information about Him? What's the difference and why does it matter?

*Brainstorm together a way that the two of you might hold each other accountable in your relationships with God. Commit to texting each other prayer requests on a regular basis.

10

The Middle

Hopefully you and your dad have worked your way through this book and have had some meaningful conversations along the way. Now that you have finally reached "the middle," we want to challenge you with one final thing and then lead you to a commitment.

Experts in educational psychology assert that you best remember the first and last things you hear. So if the first thing you read in this book is that your dad's leadership and influence is invaluable in your life, then this last thing is equally as important.

The last thing we want to leave you with is something we have hinted at several times over the past 100 pages. But just in case you missed it, we want to be perfectly clear as we come to a close.

Your dad needs to know that you believe in him.

As a gender, men are typically insecure. Beneath the confident exterior that they try to present to the world, most men walk through life secretly asking this question of the cosmos: "Do I have what it takes?"

They wonder if they have what it takes to be successful in life and in work and with their families. And while work usually provides them with tangible feedback regarding their performance (completed projects and paychecks and promotions), fathers don't have much of a grading system. Honestly, until they launch a fully-grown adult into the world at 21 or 22, they have no clue how they are doing.

That's why it's so important for you to tell him that he's a good dad. That he's a good man. He needs to know that, despite his shortcomings, he is doing a good job. He needs to confidently know that, of all the dads out there, you would choose him. Men thrive on this type of encouragement and affirmation. It is like the air they breathe.

You can see this in the movies men love. The hero is always looking to the woman in his life for affirmation. In the final, climatic scene, it is as if all he accomplished in the story is meaningless until the girl gives her nod of approval.

Watch the last ten minutes of any sports movie and you see this. "Rocky," "Glory Road," "Warrior," "Friday Night Lights," and many others have this theme. The man always looks into the crowd to see the joy on his wife's face. And while it's usually his wife, the truth holds true for daughters, as well. "Moneyball" illustrates this beautifully. Brad Pitt plays a successful baseball manager who turns down a highly lucrative job just so he can stay close to his daughter.

You can even see this in the blood and guts movies he enjoys like "Gladiator" or "Saving Private Ryan." A man may save the world in some way, but if his girl doesn't affirm him and celebrate him for what he did, the victory is empty. Men desperately need the women in their lives to communicate, "I am proud of you."

Your affirmation brings out the best in him.

So what do you do if your dad is sort of checked out? How do you affirm a dad who has been something of a disappointment to you? First of all, remember that no dad is perfect. They are all just making it up as they go along. But secondly, you need to know that one of the best ways to transform him is to build him up.

Because they are insecure, men tend to gravitate to places where they can be successful. Unfortunately, that's why many men invest too much time in work and not enough time into their families. It's because they know they can win there. If they don't feel adequate at home, their tendency is to disengage. But you have the power to change that.

Judges chapter 6 tells the story of a man named Gideon. While a battle was waging between God's people and their enemies, Gideon gave every indication that he was not interested in fighting. God's angel came to him and called him a "mighty warrior." Gideon, a self-proclaimed weakling, thought that the angel had the wrong guy. Still, God communicated to Gideon, "You are mighty." And you know what happened? Gideon rose to the occasion. He became a great warrior.

Consider the application of this for how you relate to your dad. If your words and attitude communicate that your dad is a clueless idiot, then that is probably all he will be to you. But if your words and attitude communicate that he is an awesome dad and that he has what it takes, he will believe it. And he will move towards becoming it. You have no idea how much influence you have.

Make it your goal to regularly let your father know that he is a good man. Tell him that you love him. Remind him how important he is to you. I know you probably believe this on most days, but he won't know it unless you tell him.

WHAT YOUR "BIG SISTERS" WANT YOU TO KNOW

Throughout this book, we have included lots of insights and quotes from some young women in their twenties who have made it through their teen years and come out the other side relatively well. They are like big sisters who have tried to coach you through this season of your life.

Now that they have gotten to a place where they are actually crazy about their dads again, they have some things to remind you of. Know that their wisdom is valuable to you, even if you don't fully buy into it right now. Trust us.... they know what they are talking about. Here's what they want to tell you:

> *"I hate that I was often hard to love as a teenager. Let the man who loves you most into your life! Don't distance yourself from him."*

> *"Your dad is trying his best. If you want grace from him, you need to be willing to give him some, too."*

"Get good at affirming your dad. It is great practice for marriage."

"You may not always like his rules, but he knows things you don't know. Trust him, even if you don't agree with him."

"The older I get, the more I realize that my dad was right most of the time."

"He is probably the man who will walk you down the aisle at your wedding. Don't do anything now that will give you any regrets on that day."

"Don't forget that your dad is a real person. He has feelings just like you do. You can choose to either build him up or tear him down."

Believe it or not, after you get through your teenage years, your dad will feel more like a friend and less like a parent. Sure, he will always be your father, but the pressure will be off for him to lead you and he can just love you without so many complications. Until then, know that this beautiful shift in your relationship is something that you can look forward to.

They say that you will succeed at the things you work at, so be sure to continue working on your relationship with your dad. The more attention you both give to seeking God's help and to doing it right, the more joy you will have along the way.

MAKE A CLEAR COMMITMENT

We called this book "Meet Me in the Middle" because we feel it takes work to keep you and your father connected. It requires you to selflessly move out of your comfort zone into his world and it requires him to do the same. We hope that you have found that middle ground through some of the conversations you have had.

Our hope and prayer is that the lines of communication will stay open between the two of you throughout your lives. Don't let anything get in the way of that! With that in mind, we invite you to conclude this experience by making a commitment to God and to each other.

Turn over to page 103 to find the "suitable for framing" promise to your dad. Since it will be something you give to him, carefully cut it out of the book. (Cut as deep into the margin as you can so that you can trim it and fit it into a 5X7 frame.) Sign your name at the bottom, and give it to your dad as a pledge of your unconditional love for him. If you want, write a personal note on the back of what will go in the frame (page 104). He won't see the personal note every day, but it will serve as a valuable keepsake to him in the future.

Be sure to give him a big hug when you give it to him. Dads like that sort of thing.

A Word From the Authors:

If working through this book with your dad has been a good thing in your relationship with him, we would love to hear your story. Take a minute to tell us more about it and to give a little bit of help and encouragement to other dads and daughters. Find us at www.facebook.com/MeetMeintheMiddleBook/

A Promise to My Dad:

From my earliest memories, you have been a source of strength in my life. I love being daddy's girl.

You have no idea the place you have in my heart and life. Much of who I am is because of who you are and how you have raised me.

I want to be strong, but sometimes I feel very fragile. Thank you for being a tender warrior who fights for my heart and God's very best in my life.

If I ever seem to push you away, it doesn't mean I don't need you. I will always need you. Just give me a little space and then try again later.

I pray that you will always guard your heart and stay close to our heavenly Father. I'm counting on you to show me the way.

You are not a perfect dad, but you're a pretty good one. Of all the dads in the world, I would choose you. You have what it takes. I believe in you.

My love for you is unconditional. There is nothing you can ever do that will make me love you any more or any less.

_____

A Personal Note for My Dad:

You hold in your hands a very special book.

Start here and it's a book for dads. Flip it over and it's a book for girls aged 12-19. Both of the books cover the same 10 critical conversations that fathers and daughters need to have during the challenging teen years.

As dad and daughter pass this book back and forth, they end up talking about identity, faith, friends, beauty, boys, sex, porn, and their desperate need to stay connected to one another during the teen years. Because they have to share, it forces them to keep the dialogue open about what they are reading and learning.

Finally, the two books literally meet in the middle. In the center of the book, dad and daughter will find a commitment. It's a pledge to stay connected and to offer unconditional love to each other, serving as a constant reminder of how important the father/daughter relationship will always be.

Stay close to your daughter. Keep talking to her.

Meet her in the middle.

Barrett and Jenifer Johnson

are the founders of I.N.F.O. for Families, a ministry committed to helping Imperfect and Normal Families navigate our hyper-sexualized culture. The authors of *The Talks* and *The Young Man's Guide to Awesomeness*, they have raised five kids (including three daughters) and have been married for 28 years.

www.INFOforFamilies.com

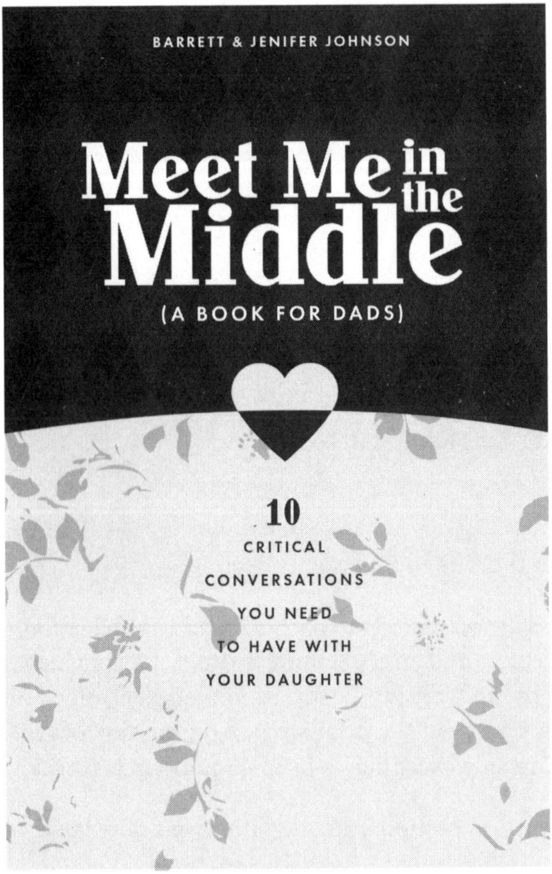

Meet Me in the Middle

BARRETT & JENIFER JOHNSON

Meet Me in the Middle

(A BOOK FOR DADS)

10 CRITICAL CONVERSATIONS YOU NEED TO HAVE WITH YOUR DAUGHTER

Also from Barrett and Jenifer Johnson:

The Talks

Your Imperfect & Normal Family

The Young Man's Guide to Awesomeness

INFO FOR FAMILIES resources

Meet Me in the Middle

Cover Design by Lucas Bauer.

For Lindsey, Emilie, and Maddie Kate.

May you always desire to walk with your heavenly Father, in spite of the imperfect example you had in your earthly one.

Contents

Introduction

Hi, there!

If you're reading these words right now, it's because you are a dad who loves his daughter. You want to connect with her heart and to coach her as she walks through what can be a difficult season: the teenage years.

If that's you, welcome! If, on the other hand, you are a teenage girl reading these words, you're reading the wrong half of this book. Simply flip it over and start there. If you are neither a dad nor a girl, then go read something else. There's nothing for you here.

We have created this unique resource to get fathers and their daughters talking about some important topics. Adolescence is a time when your daughter desperately needs your guidance and protection. Hopefully, this book will connect the hearts of you and your daughter and "tee

up" some critical conversations you should have.

If you haven't already noticed, what you're holding right now is actually two books. One is for you and one is for your daughter. They both cover the same content, but they come at it from two different perspectives: what you need to know and what your daughter needs to know.

Because it's two books in one, you're going to have to share. You should read a chapter and then let your daughter read the corresponding chapter in her half of the book. Then you have to carve out some time to talk about what you have read.

We called this thing *Meet Me in the Middle* for a couple of reasons.

The first is because we know that dads and daughters can sometimes have a hard time finding the neutral ground to connect. If you're going to stay close to your girl during this season, you're going to have to "meet her in the middle" and get into her world a bit. We know that's not always the easiest thing to do. But you are going to have to make an attempt to see things from your daughter's perspective.

And don't worry, in the book for daughters, we're telling her to do the exact same thing, encouraging her to see things from your viewpoint.

The other reason we called this book *Meet Me in the Middle* is because of the way the two books are laid out. If you notice, both of you start from your side of the book and then your reading eventually takes you to the middle. Once you are all done, we encourage you to make the commitment that you find there. But there's no rush. Work through the book and get there when you get there.

There is something else you will see as you read. As we were writing this, we interviewed a bunch of 20-something young women. They were some girls we know who have already made it through their teenage years, but who still have good (and raw) memories of what it was like to be a teenager. We took their insights and tweaked their words to make their voices sound like they were coming from your teenage daughter. Their words should serve as excellent clues as to exactly what your daughter needs from you right now. Their perspectives are absolute gold, so don't skip over them. **You will see them in bold type like this.**

One more thing: this is not just a static "read the words" book. (Most men don't like that kind of book anyway.) This thing is meant to be interactive. There will be places to respond to questions and to share some thoughts with your daughter. There are also some suggested activities to help you to connect with her. So don't just read this book. Experience it! We suggest that you both read it one chapter at a time. Then sit down together and talk about what you have read.

We sincerely hope that working through this book with your daughter will help you to effectively pass on God's perspective on a bunch of stuff you know she is dealing with. And if she's not quite dealing with it yet, she probably will be sooner or later.

Hopefully, you'll be closer to your daughter than ever before as you work through this together. We pray that God does some incredible things in your relationship with her!

-Barrett and Jenifer Johnson

1

Your Daughter

Sometimes, you hear a powerful truth from an unlikely source.

In 2003, John Mayer was a voice of poetic insight when he won a Grammy for his song "Daughters." I suppose if God can speak through a donkey, he can speak through a rock star.

In the song, Mayer sings about his frustration in trying to understand the emotional ups and downs of the girl he is dating. He describes her as a "maze where all of the walls continually change." He finally concludes that it's not because of him; it's because of the girl's father. He goes on to say (in part):

Fathers, be good to your daughters.
Daughters will love like you do...

Oh, you see that skin?
It's the same she's been standing in
Since the day she saw him walking away,
Now she's left cleaning up the mess he made.

On behalf of every man
Looking out for every girl
You are the God and weight of her world.

So fathers, be good to your daughters
Daughters will love like you do.

It is impossible to quantify the impact of the father-daughter relationship. While you might be tempted to think that what you do has little impact, the opposite is true. Sure, your daughter values her mother, but she desperately needs her father.

You probably have fond memories of those years when your daughter was "daddy's girl." Before adolescence arrived, she thought you hung the moon and likely had you securely wrapped around her finger. She needed and wanted your affection and attention.

Then something changed. She started growing up. She took an interest in makeup and music. She got a few curves. Your little girl is little no longer.

If you're like most dads, this transition that every girl goes through marks a turning point in your relationship with her. Some dads don't make the adjustments needed to continue to stay close to their daughters. The result is that their daughters pull away from them. Most dads let them go, failing to adjust to the new normal.

But what if that awkward shift in your relationship is not

her pulling away? What if she's just growing up? What if she still desperately wants you in her life, just in a different way?

WHY YOUR RELATIONSHIP WITH YOUR DAUGHTER (STILL) MATTERS

As she moves through the tumultuous waters of her teenage years, there will be many days (and months and years) when your daughter won't know which way is up. Hormonal changes will do a number on her. She will struggle to find out who she is in her peer relationships, in her family, and in God's big picture. She will need her dad to help her to find her way.

Girls seek male approval just as boys want the admiration of the women in their lives. And it all starts with dad. There is a special bond there like no other. If that relationship is solid, it has the power to be the most important and influential one in her life. If dad says she is loved, valuable, intelligent, and beautiful, then she is. Granted, she may doubt it at times, but if his voice is consistent, she will come to believe it. And that's the sort of stuff that sticks with a girl for life. (Heads-up! Here's the first quote from a girl who is probably a lot like your daughter.)

"Dad, I know I can be hard to like. I get it. On many days, I have a hard time liking myself. But that's when I need you the most."

The stakes get even higher when it comes to how your daughter views God. While you are certainly not the "God of her world," as John Mayer sings, you will, in a big part,

7

give her a picture of what God is like. Most children and teenagers create a picture of their heavenly Father based on what they see in their earthly fathers. This impression can evolve and change over time, but dads set the pace. (No pressure or anything, dad.)

THE LIE THAT GIRLS BELIEVE ABOUT THEIR DADS

As your daughter makes the transition into adolescence, a lot of different sources will begin to tell her a lie. Both the media she ingests, and many of the friends she interacts with will tell her the same thing: "Your dad is clueless."

She is likely to begin believing that you are irrelevant. That you can't possibly understand what she is going through. That you can't relate. The ironic thing is that as she is beginning to experience more "adult" issues, she is likely to start thinking that you – one of the key adults in her life – don't have anything to offer.

Why do so many teenage girls get the wrong idea that their dads no longer matter? It's because so many dads do check out during a season when they are needed more than ever. Their daughters become too complicated, too emotional, and too dramatic. Connecting with her used to be easy and now it's an incredible challenge. Too many dads give up, so most girls out there aren't wrong. Their dads have become irrelevant, after all. But that's not you. You're going to be different.

> *"Dad, I might communicate to you that I don't care about you opinion, but if you don't share your opinion, then I think that you don't care about me."*

THE TRUTH YOUR DAUGHTER DESPERATELY NEEDS TO KNOW

Yes, she is changing, and yes, she is more of a mystery than ever before. But she still needs you. She may not seem as interested when you try to connect with her, but she still has a longing to know and be known by her father.

During this time, she needs to know that you are there for her. She needs your emotional and physical presence in her life. Yes, things have changed and it's going to be harder than ever before, but you need to step up and convince her that, for better or worse, she is stuck with you.

Note that this has nothing to do with knowing exactly what she is going through or having all the answers for her problems. Because, let's face it, you don't know what it feels like to be a teenage girl. You can listen, try to empathize, and maybe offer some wisdom, but you're never going to fully get it. None of that matters. From your daughter's perspective, you trying and failing is a lot worse than you not trying at all. So don't give up.

> *"Dad, it's okay if you don't feel like you know what you're doing as a dad. You still have to show up. The effort you make in love still feels like love."*

During these years, what she needs most from you is your presence. The day will one day come when she will relate to your perspective and advice, but that day is not here yet. In the meantime, you're going to have to wait it out and strive to be connected to her. As her body changes, her emotions mature, and she begins to grow into a woman, you can't afford to bail on her. You are still relevant.

God gave the prophet Ezekiel a story to tell about how He cares for His people. As you will see, it is particularly relevant to fathers and daughters. Found in Ezekiel 16, it goes something like this:

A baby is born in secret and then abandoned in a field. The baby girl is left alone to die, unfed and uncared for, writhing around in a pool of blood. God saw that the baby was unloved and alone and had intense compassion for her. From that moment, God took responsibility for her life and her well-being, speaking life and blessings on her, just as any good parent naturally does.

The story goes on that the girl eventually matured sexually. The Bible says that her breasts were formed and her hair grew long and beautiful, yet she was still naked. I love what is described in verse 8: *"Later I passed by, and when I looked at you and saw that you were old enough for love, I spread the corner of my garment over you and covered your naked body."*

God models for fathers the kind of care and protection that our daughters need. When their bodies begin to mature and their hearts begin to awaken to love, our girls need their fathers' care more than ever before.

HELPING HER TO BE DIFFERENT

God has called you to step into this vital role with your girl. It takes hard work, but here are few places to start...

1. Be a Tender Warrior

If you're still interacting with your teenager exactly like you did when she was ten, then you're going to have to change

your approach. We'll talk a lot about that in the coming chapters, but one characteristic of your role as father needs to be consistent: you must parent your daughter as much like Jesus as possible.

Author Stu Weber writes that men should strive to be "tender warriors." That's the perfect description of Jesus. He was simultaneously gentle and fierce. His love was rooted in both truth and empathy. Most importantly, Jesus was present with those He loved. Our daughters need us to be present with this kind of strong passion for them.

Your daughter should see you as tender, a man with whom she can share her feelings without fear of judgment. She needs to feel close to you, emotionally. She should also see you as a strong protector, one who would make sacrifices and take great risks to fight for her. She needs to know that you would not hesitate to lay down your life for her.

> *"Don't be a robotic man with all the answers. Be a real person. That means you sometimes have to just let me feel emotional and be frustrated at times."*

2. Nurture Your Relationship with Her

Experts agree that one of the biggest mistakes parents can make is striving too hard to be their child's buddy. The result for some has been an extreme swing in the opposite direction: dads who actually make it their goal to remain emotionally disconnected from their children. As one father I heard put it: "My goal with my teenagers is to make sure they don't like me." I think he is missing the point.

Regarding the father/daughter relationship, I once heard

this good advice about your teenagers: "You want them to like you. If they don't like you, they won't listen to you. After all, do you listen to people that you don't like?" You know that you don't.

Dads can never stop pursuing a love relationship with their daughters. And yes, I know, it used to come so easy. Just face the facts that this is going to be a challenge at times. It would be wise to speak her "love language," the unique way she best hears love.

Author Gary Chapman names five of them: words of affirmation, quality time, giving gifts, physical touch, and acts of service. Learn her language and speak it regularly. You may have to double or triple your efforts to connect at an emotional level with your girl during the teen years, but know that it is worth it.

3. Be a Voice of Truth

Throughout her life, your daughter will be bombarded with plenty of bad information about who she is, what is important, and where she should invest her energies. She is particularly susceptible to believing this bad information during her formative teen years. That's why you have to be engaged enough to pick up on the lies and be ready to remind her of the truth.

> *"Don't feel obligated to make everything you share with me this big dramatic event. Just share truth with me as we go along with life. Don't make it weird."*

More important than just responding to lies with truths, you would do well to be as "pre-emptive" as possible. As you parent your daughter, you should be constantly

sharing God's truth and perspective about life issues with her. That way, when she encounters a lie in her world, she will know better. You have prepared her for what she will face.

Know this: rarely will she thank you. When you are communicating a value or a reality that you know is important for her to know, don't expect to hear, "Thanks, Dad, for sharing this vital truth that I know will serve me well in life!" In contrast, you can expect blank stares and the occasional eye roll. But just because she doesn't respond with enthusiasm, doesn't mean that she's not hearing you.

MEET YOUR DAUGHTER IN THE MIDDLE

As you start reading this book together, it might feel a bit strange to have the intentional conversations we suggest here. Get things rolling by going on a simple date for ice cream or coffee. Share with your daughter how you hope to stay close to her. Confess that you sometimes feel inadequate and that you need her to offer you some grace as you parent her. During your time together, be sure to listen more than you talk. Pray that this book might be an effective tool to help keep the two of you connected. (See the next page for some specific things you can talk about.)

SOME THINGS TO TALK ABOUT

*Tell her how you might feel inadequate as a father.

*Tell her how it can sometimes be difficult to connect with her. Ask her for suggestions as to how you can do better.

*Invite her to be honest with you about her feelings and experiences. Don't evaluate or judge; just listen. If you shut her down or get defensive, she will learn that you are not a safe place to be honest.

*Allow her to grade you on your "emotional closeness" to her. Talk about how you might improve in that area.

2

Friends

If a historian attempted to identify the most evil regimes in history, I'm sure that the Nazis under Adolf Hitler would be at the top of his list. Maybe Joseph Stalin in Russia or Pol Pot in Cambodia would be in the top 10. But, in terms of cruelty alone, somewhere on the list you might find the mean girls that your daughter has to interact with every day. Of course that's a stretch, but it's pretty bad.

Teenage girls have the power to bring hurt and suffering to each other like nothing else in our culture. Of course, they don't kill millions of people like an evil dictator might, but the emotional wounds they inflict on each other can feel incredibly real and raw. Add to that the fact that adolescence is one of the most tender and emotionally fragile seasons of a girl's life, and it's a very big deal.

While there may be a few bullies or "mean girls" who are

creating the culture and dolling out the hurt to everyone else, few girls escape this season unscathed. Even those with tough exteriors and confident personalities get wounded regularly by their peers. One young woman we interviewed used a colorful expletive to describe how bad it is during middle school and much of high school.

"Girls and their friends are incredibly messy. It's an absolute (bleep) show."

This pain is something that most guys don't have much experience with. We're not as emotional in our personal relationships, and quite frankly, we don't care about this stuff like girls do. But as a dad who wants to stay connected with his daughter, you have to realize the scope of what your girl is going through. And then you have to try to help her manage it.

WHY FRIENDSHIPS MATTER

You might be tempted to minimize this issue by declaring, "Your friend drama will blow over! You'll get through it! Stop worrying about it so much!" Attractive –and obvious – as that strategy might be to you, it is not an option. What your daughter feels about this stuff is real. It is perhaps the most real thing in her life. And these issues are not going to disappear just because you think they are trivial.

As a girl makes the transition from childhood to adulthood, she starts trying to find herself and her identity not in the context of the family she has known, but in the larger world out there. She is asking, "Who am I apart from my parents?" While she will hopefully find the answer to that

question in God's eyes, for now, she is more likely to look to her peers.

> *"It feels like the girls I interact with are my whole world, so what they do impacts me to the core."*

Sure, her friends are a fickle, clueless, and unreliable bunch, but it is what she knows. The result is that what they say about her, how she fits in, and where she lands in the social order all define her reality. Her friends are often the voices she hears the loudest and they are very, very persuasive.

Add to that the fact that her adolescent brain has not yet learned to manage the stress in her life, and the problem is compounded. On a scale of 1 to 10, the stress of a difficult friendship might be a 3 in your mind, but to her, it's a 27. It literally feels as stressful and as overwhelming as what you might feel if you were simultaneously losing your job, caring for a dying parent, and getting a cancer diagnosis. It truly feels that big to her.

THE LIE THAT GIRLS BELIEVE ABOUT FRIENDS

While teenagers from every generation have had to deal with "mean girls," smartphones have multiplied their impact. Your girl has probably never known what it is like to interact with her post-pubescent peers apart from social media. This is huge. The constant connection she has with her friends means that they will have constant influence on her life.

Your daughter will likely believe what her phone indirectly tells her. In the course of any given day, it's likely that your girl will send and receive hundreds of texts, be tagged in dozens of pictures, and check her phone for social media updates 50 to 100 times a day. If she took a selfie of what she wore to school that day, she will (unknowingly) evaluate her worth as an individual based upon how many people "liked" her photo. Sadly, she may even think that she actually has 1,250 friends.

"With social media, I know what is happening with my peers the minute it happens. FOMO (the Fear Of Missing Out) can be crippling."

Since her peers, including the mean ones, have access to the same platforms, it's a free-for-all. Anyone can say anything to anybody. Something that a dad would see as benign can be devastating to a teenage girl. Her friend might post a picture of a group and then tag some of the girls (her way of saying "look at us!") but not include others. It's a purposeful slam that is subtle but enormous from your girl's point of view.

THE TRUTH YOUR DAUGHTER DESPERATELY NEEDS TO KNOW

Many people have lost sight of any sense of identity that is rooted in our fundamental value as children of God, created in His image with eternal purpose and meaning. Instead, we look to the affirmations of others on our phones in the form of follows, likes, clicks, and comments. When it comes to navigating her relationships with her

peers, your daughter needs to know you are there for her. She needs to have a sense that you are in her corner. She needs to know that you are a strong, stable force of love in her life when everyone else seems to be completely unreliable.

> *"You don't have to solve my girlfriend problems. I know you're not equipped for that. But I need you to remind me that I'm strong and good and that I will eventually get through it."*

One day she will come out the other side of this season and not be so powerfully impacted by all the girl drama. But she's in it now and there are no easy solutions. You just have to get her through it. It may take a few years of you learning to patiently listen and empathize with her pain, but she will get through it. In the meantime, your presence will help.

In Galatians 1:10, Paul asks a rhetorical question. With his strong personality and blunt writing, you can be sure that he is making an important point. He asks, *"Am I now trying to win the approval of human beings, or of God? Or am I trying to please people?"*

Paul suggests that striving for the approval of other people will almost always lead to disappointment. And even if your daughter were to pull it off and be incredibly popular with everyone, she's probably not doing it by pleasing God. We can't please both God and people. None of us can have both. That's not how it works.

It may take her a while to learn this lesson, but she can also be sure that where God is always reliable, her friends (no

matter how great they are) will eventually let her down. Proverbs 18:24 says, *"There are 'friends' who destroy each other, but a real friend sticks closer than a brother."* God is close, even if your daughter's friends abandon her. She needs to have the sense that you are close, too.

> *"If I'm going through a tough time, just bring me flowers or something. Show me you care."*

One way that your daughter will learn about the faithfulness of God is in the faithfulness of her earthly father. Flawed as you are, you are giving your kids the clearest picture of what God is like. Needless to say, there's a lot riding on you, dad.

HELPING YOUR DAUGHTER MANAGE CHALLENGING FRIENDSHIPS

1. Listen and Empathize

As with most of the interactions you have with the women in your life, you're going to have to lay down your impulse to "fix it." When you sense that your daughter is feeling the pain of a difficult relationship, don't work the problem. This is a big stretch, but do your best to identify with what she is going through and then offer her some compassion and understanding.

> *"Dad, if I confide in you about my friend junk, don't feel obligated to solve my problem. Just say nice things. That's enough."*

You are allowed to admit that you don't get it, but don't belittle her experience. Just say something like, "I don't know what you are going through, but I know it's hard on you." If she invites you into it, you can help brainstorm with her some possible solutions to how to work through it. Don't tell her what to do. Instead, help her to learn the skills to manage the relationships she is likely to face throughout her entire life.

2. Guard Social Media

Girls in our culture like posting pictures of themselves online. While she may be simply looking for some positive affirmation, there is always the possibility that she will get a cruel comment from someone who wants to hurt her. Or she may hear "crickets," which might have an altogether different effect on her self-esteem.

Stay in touch with what your daughter does online. As her father, you have every right to know what sites she is on and to follow her. You also have every right to know her passwords and to examine her phone at any time. Setting these parameters when your daughter is young will help avoid a lot of conflict down the road.

And if you haven't had the digital footprint conversation yet, then that's long overdue. One out of every three teen girls has sent a sexually explicit picture of themselves to someone. This stuff is happening more than you think, so you have to talk about it.

3. Have Her Back

As she interacts with her friends, there will be plenty of

other girls who will cause your daughter to question her worth and even her sanity. It can sometimes feel to her like the whole world is against her. In those moments, nothing will give her confidence like having the sense that someone is on her side. That someone should be you.

You may be tempted to rush in and intervene in the midst of her friend drama. (Your daughter's mother will probably be even more impulsive in that area.) There may be rare occasions when that is necessary, but most of your daughter's challenges will be better served by you staying out. Instead of swooping in and trying to solve her problems for her, help her to cope with the complications of friendship in our modern world. What is important is that she knows that you would rescue her if she needed you.

MEET YOUR DAUGHTER IN THE MIDDLE

Admit to her that you don't fully understand how friendships are lived online in social media. Invite her to show you her Instagram or Snapchat feed. Ask her what types of things she scans for on her friends' posts. Get her to tell you what emotions she feels when she sees different types of posts from her friends or even her "frenemies."

SOME THINGS TO TALK ABOUT

*Ask her what difficult people and conflicts she is dealing with in her social circles right now.

*Ask your daughter if any girls out there would see her actions (on social media or in the real world) as cruel or insensitive. Discuss what she might do to diffuse any drama she has created.

*Invite her to share ideas about how you can best love and help her as she deals with sometimes challenging friendships.

3

Identity

Every person in our culture lives in a constant state of comparison. We compare our looks, our stuff, our grades, our performance, our accomplishments, and just about everything else that a capitalistic society offers.

The scorecards are different for the various arenas of life. Some, like our grades in school or our income in the workplace, are tangible. Some are less clear, like our social status or our looks. Sadly, in our modern world, social media has enabled what used to be abstract to become much more concrete. As we move further and further in that direction, our girls will suffer more and more.

The Netflix series Black Mirror recently characterized this beautifully in an episode called "Nosedive." In the near future where status is clearly tracked and scored online, a woman's life collapses when she can't earn enough points to climb the social ladder as she wishes. It was a troubling

show to watch, but it seemed somehow familiar. The awful future it showed was the future we are headed for.

From the time your daughter was little, she has been trying to find her place in the world. How she fits in with her friends dictates much about how she feels about herself. Because of the technology she is so comfortable with, she constantly compares herself to others, trying to measure herself based upon unrealistic ideals of success, happiness, beauty, and popularity. Rarely does she measure up.

Because her life is lived out on social media, her perceived inadequacies and insecurities are there for everyone to see. No matter how popular she might be, she is left feeling inadequate at best and bullied at the worst. She is in desperate need to find her identity in something bigger than herself.

WHY IDENTITY MATTERS

Psychologists typically agree that much of a person's self-esteem is formed by age 12. It can certainly grow and shift after that, but much of what is established during childhood is solidified through the teenage years. If you are a dad who is paying attention, you might see the important part you play in her story.

Through her childhood, your daughter has probably gotten the message that she is pretty, kind, worthy, and valuable. She likely has internal doubts, but she generally believes it because it's the primary message she has received for her entire life. Then she goes to middle school. Tossed into that powder keg, she is suddenly bombarded with messages that run contrary to the narrative she has heard all her life. She's ugly. She's lame. She doesn't measure up.

*"There are many days where I totally hate who
I am. I literally can't stand myself."*

It is during this noisy season that she needs to continue to clearly and consistently hear the message that God wants to speak over her. This season is critical and this message is vital because her tender heart can easily believe the nonsense that the world is screaming at her.

THE LIE THAT GIRLS BELIEVE ABOUT THEIR VALUE

In hundreds of different forms, your daughter is going to hear the lie that has been spoken to humanity since the serpent spoke it to Adam. The fundamental lie is that God is not enough for you. You need more than Him to find your worth. While this lie takes on many forms, your daughter's tender mind is likely to believe one of several versions of it.

In *The Search for Significance*, author Robert McGee summarizes the lie into four things, all of which are rooted in our wrong belief that our self worth is based upon our performance and the opinions of others. If you're not careful, you can inadvertently cause your daughter to believe these lies as you parent her.

1. The Performance Trap:
"I must meet certain standards to feel good about myself."

2. The Approval Addict:
"I must be approved by certain others to feel good about myself."

3. The Blame Game:

"Those who fail are unworthy of love and deserve to be punished."

4. Shame:

"I am what I am. I cannot change. I am hopeless."

Just about every struggle your daughter is going to have during her teen years can be traced back to the first three lies listed above. Peer pressure, temptation, identity crises, discipline issues, and just about anything else you find in adolescence are rooted in these things. If she is unable to embrace God's truth about who she is, she might come to believe lie #4 about shame. This is not God's desire for her. He wants her to know all that He has done to rescue her from these lies.

"Don't just praise me when I accomplish something. I need your affirmation just because."

THE TRUTH YOUR DAUGHTER DESPERATELY NEEDS TO KNOW

Perhaps the most important thing you can teach your daughter is to find her place in God's big story. To do that, she is going to have to love Him, learn to hear His voice, and follow His leading in her life. This won't happen by just going to church and seeing faith as just one more part of the American Dream. If she doesn't find her identity in Christ, she will end up looking in all the wrong places.

Many of our girls never fall in love with Jesus or find Him to be altogether satisfying. They have an intense longing to

connect, to be needed, to be loved...all longings that only God can satisfy. Unfortunately, many girls bypass their Creator (God) and look to the created (other people) to try to get these deepest needs met. Left unchecked, many will one day look to a man to "complete" them.

A girl like this will eventually stand at an altar, making her vows, pledging her life and her future to her groom. If she hasn't first found her identity in Christ, what she is really saying is this: "I'm counting on you to give my life purpose. I'm depending on you to give me my identity and meaning in life. I'm counting on you to meet my every need."

Dads must teach their daughters that their worth and purpose and identity can never be found in another person. It can only be found in the person of Jesus Christ. They need to be regularly reminded that they have value because of who their Creator says they are. Only when your girl embraces this can she begin to develop a lasting and healthy self-image.

> *"Nobody is teaching me how to love myself. Everybody assumes I'm going to figure it out on my own. "*

The Bible is full of words that tell us who we are as a result of all that God has done for us. These things literally define a Christian's identity. While all of us struggle with believing these things are true, teenage girls have a particularly hard time embracing them. Your daughter needs to be reminded of these realities often. Dad, you're just the guy to tell her that she...

- Is God's child (John 1:12)

- Is Christ's friend (John 15:15)

- Belongs to God (I Corinthian 6:19-20)

- Is a saint; a holy one (Ephesians 1:1)

- Is free from condemnation (Romans 8:1-2)

- Cannot be separated from God's love (Romans 8:35-39)

- Has been redeemed and forgiven (Colossians 1:14)

- Is a citizen of Heaven (Philippians 3:20)

- Can approach God with confidence (Ephesians 3:12)

- Is complete in Christ (Colossians 2:10)

If this is who God declares your daughter to be, then this is who she is! Unlike just about everything else in life, she doesn't have to earn this new identity. Because of Jesus, those who have trusted in Him have been given spiritual birth as children of God.

> *"Right now, I feel the need to constantly change and shift who I am to make people like me. I will need your help if I'm going to stop this madness and start seeing myself as God sees me."*

Like nothing else your daughter will struggle with, the issue of her value before God is fundamental. How she sees herself will play out in the battlefield of her mind and will impact every aspect of her life.

Most dads will insist that they make this better for their daughters, not worse. But our experience shows that the

perspective of many girls is that they have a hard time pleasing their dads. What they do is never quite good enough for him. This fuels the "performance trap" and leads to shame.

Girls desire their dads' approval but few feel like they have it. This inevitably extends to their relationship with God, and they can end up seeing Him as one they can never please. Dad, you have the power to change this for your daughter! This is where your good intentions are meaningless and your words mean everything.

HELPING HER TO BE DIFFERENT

1. Watch for Wrong Thinking

While you can never know every thought she has and every lie she believes about her identity, you still must pay attention. These things are happening to her so you must ask God for wisdom to notice. If her behavior radically shifts or some negative emotions rise to the surface, it may be a sign of wrong thinking.

Comparison will do that if she feels she doesn't measure up in some situation. Her need for acceptance from her peers will spike if she is left out of something. She may come to believe that she is a bad person and enter into a state of "I'm so lonely and nobody loves me." If you see external signs that these things are happening to her heart, ask God for wisdom on how to help build her up. Then boldly insert yourself (and your words) into her life.

2. Affirm Her Unique Strengths

God has gifted every person with unique gifts that are there

both for God's glory and, by extension, for our joy as we exercise them. Unfortunately, our world has its own scorecard that tends to value certain strengths over others. During adolescence, many parents inadvertently communicate to kids that their grades are all that matter because that's the main thing that we hold them accountable for. We need to do better than that.

Find those areas where your daughter is gifted and celebrate those things. Give her chances to grow and flourish in those areas. As James Dobson says, "A kid who doesn't know what she is good at will start to wonder what she is good for." This can be a key to beginning to find her place in God's big story. Even if her interests are radically different from your interests, celebrate how God is working in her life.

3. When She Fails, Remind Her of Who She Is

If she blows it (and she will blow it), there will probably be a place for discipline or a consequence for her behavior. But if you give punishment without offering her a better way, she will learn that the lies of the "blame game" are true. She's a bad person and punishment is all she deserves.

Instead, remind her that what she did or how she acted is not who she was meant to be. Remind her of the truth of who God has made her to be in Christ. Remind her of her identity found in Him. "This is who you are, now let's start acting like it."

"Treating me like I am precious and valuable will communicate that I have worth more powerfully than anything else you do."

Before she was your daughter, she was a child of God. In most of our cases, she will still be a child of God long after we are dead and gone. That is why your goal should be to push her into Jesus so she grows in dependence upon Him far more than she is dependent upon you. Only when she finds her place and her identity in Him will her heart and life begin to flourish as God intended from the beginning.

MEET YOUR DAUGHTER IN THE MIDDLE

Identify something that she really loves to do; a passion that God has placed in her heart. Plan an outing that enables you to experience that thing with her. If she is into sports, go to a game. If she is creative, go to a pottery place together. If she loves to invest in others, find a ministry where you can serve together for a few hours. As you enjoy your time together, look for opportunities to affirm who God has made her to be.

SOME THINGS TO TALK ABOUT

*Tell her about some of the first times you noticed the unique personality traits in her younger self.

*Share what it means for you to know that you are fully loved by God, regardless of what you do. Confess the times when it is hard to believe that truth.

*Read through the list of truths about our identity in Christ from a few pages back. Discuss the implications of each of them.

*Ask: "How can I remind you that you have worth apart from what you do? Do I do anything that makes you think that you have to earn God's love? Or my love?"

4

Beauty

There is a private, internal conflict that every girl is constantly wrestling with. As much as a dad might try to minimize the impact of this struggle in his daughter, it seems to be hard-wired into the female brain. She desperately wants to know the answer to this question:

"Am I beautiful?"

This shows up early in the preschool years, fueled in most girls by a steady diet of Disney princess movies and Barbies. It develops further during later childhood, as she begins to notice her peers and begins to start comparing herself to others. By the time your girl reaches adolescence, it's fully developed as one of the central themes of her subconscious brain. (Note to husbands: it is very likely that your wife is still asking that question. You need to help her to answer it.)

You might be tempted to write this off as a superficial issue that your daughter will eventually overcome, but it's not that simple. Our culture's pre-occupation with external beauty is the very culture that your daughter is immersed in. Unfortunately, her understanding of how she fits in and measures up has the power to significantly impact her life. What you communicate to her in this area has incredible weight.

WHY HER VIEW OF BEAUTY MATTERS

There are a few dozen supermodels who are setting the pace for what is beautiful in our culture. Sadly, the perfect standard they set for our girls is totally unrealistic. (Note: they rely heavily on Photoshop.) To make things even harder on our girls, the culture's definition of beauty keeps changing.

When fashion styles evolve, your girl can go out and buy something new. When our world's definition of what is beautiful evolves, all it does is add to the burden on her. She can't change her curves or her hair as easily as her clothes. The powers that be can easily roll out some new models who fit the standard, but the girls in your life will never be able to keep up.

"I'm constantly asking the question, 'Am I pretty?' I hear a lot of voices giving me answers. Dad, I really need to hear yours."

For that reason, your daughter must gain, and then maintain, a healthy view of her beauty. Sure, she will always spend some time working on her appearance, but what she really needs is a God-given perspective of the fact that she

is *"wonderfully made."* This belief and confidence can sustain her as fashion trends shift and change.

THE LIE THAT GIRLS BELIEVE ABOUT BEAUTY

There is a subtle but powerful message that is constantly being whispered to your daughter. It is that her appearance is what matters most. While this has been true for young women through the ages, there has been a major shift in the past decade. Today, being beautiful has been surpassed by the greater value of being "sexy."

The role models that an entire generation of young women follows are selling this brand of beauty. Sadly, our girls are buying what they are selling.

Consider the Kardashians. Before they got famous for being famous, what was their creative or cultural or intellectual contribution to society? Anyone? Their brand and the bulk of their influence are based almost entirely on their sex appeal. Their Instagram accounts are filled almost entirely with selfies, and nearly 250 million people are watching their every move.

As our daughters begin to transform into full-fledged young women, it is likely that the question they are asking has shifted from, "Am I pretty" to, "Am I sexy?" If you scan the Instagram accounts of most teenage girls today, you will likely see the same pouty faces and alluring poses that you see on the filtered photos of Kim and Khloe and Kourtney. And I guarantee that these girls regularly check the comment sections of their photos.

What are people saying? Are they answering the question

that they are crying out for the answer to: "How do I look?"

There is too much information coming into your daughter's life via her smartphone. It is setting an unrealistic standard and then giving her an unhealthy means to try to reach the standard. She even has a built in scorecard via likes and comments to see how she is measuring up. The net result is discouragement and dismay. She will probably come to believe that she's not pretty enough.

THE TRUTH YOUR DAUGHTER DESPERATELY NEEDS TO KNOW

Your teenage girl needs to hear from you that she is beautiful. No matter how old she gets, this need will never go away. Even if she believes it confidently in one moment, all it takes is criticism from a peer or a comparison to someone online for self-doubt to creep in. That's why this affirmation from dad must be given frequently.

If your experience is like most dads, doing this was easy when she was younger. She would dress up in a princess costume and twirl her dress around asking, "Daddy, how do I look?" For most dads, that's an absolute no-brainer. She asks for affirmation and we give it to her. "You look beautiful, sweetheart." This becomes much harder as she gets older. Still, we must persist.

> *"There's always power when you tell me I look nice. Even if I roll my eyes, it's still welcome. Just ignore my body language and keep saying it."*

The problem lies in the fact that most girls under the age of 10 have no reason to doubt that they are pretty. When she

asks you for your opinion, she's looking for an affirmation of what she already knows to be an absolute truth. *"Yes, dad...I know....I'm beautiful."*

But something happens during the transition to the teen years. She stops believing that she is wonderfully made and starts buying into the lie that says she will never measure up. That's why your reassurance is so important.

As a girl transitions into young adulthood, she begins to search for her own identity. With all that she sees around her, your daughter needs the reassurance that she is beautiful and significant. It is at this stage that you should affirm all the positive traits you see in her, especially the inner qualities of her heart and character.

Yes, she is beautiful, but also remind her that a healthy self-image will always trump external beauty. One is temporary and the other will sustain her for life. One critically important job you have is to remind her that she is much more than the sum of her looks.

> *I love it when you say, "You make that dress look beautiful" even better than, "You look beautiful in that dress." It's a small thing, but it builds me up.*

Scripture can seem to give two contrary views about the value of a woman's beauty. On the one hand, Psalm 144:12b encourages a father to take pride in his daughter's beauty. The psalmist writes that, *"Our daughters will be like pillars carved to adorn a palace."* There is nothing wrong with celebrating the external loveliness of the fairer gender.

On the other hand, God warns us not to prioritize a

woman's beauty over the character of her heart. In I Peter 3:3-4, women are commanded, *"Don't be concerned about the outward beauty of fancy hairstyles, expensive jewelry, or beautiful clothes. You should clothe yourselves instead with the beauty that comes from within, the unfading beauty of a gentle and quiet spirit, which is so precious to God."* It is what is inside of a woman that is the most beautiful.

Both of these perspectives are found in Scripture, so both are true. The challenge your daughter faces is in finding a healthy balance. It is hard to downplay the importance of external beauty when every voice around her screams that it matters. Some of the voices are quite loud. Your job as her father is to help her to ignore the voices that say that her looks define her.

> *"Don't just affirm me when I'm all fixed up. I love it when you catch me off guard and tell me I'm beautiful just because."*

HELPING HER TO BE DIFFERENT

Your goal should be to help your girl to develop a healthy self image when it comes to her appearance. At the foundation of that is helping her to know that God has created her as a work of art; a reflection of His glory. There are a few places to start communicating that critical message.

1. Affirm All of Her

In this season when boys begin to notice girls, there's something that your daughter has probably been made

keenly aware of: girls who flaunt their bodies usually make a powerful first impression on boys. The bad news is that this first impression is likely all the boys will remember. They might get the attention, but it's rarely the attention that they want in the long run.

A good question to pose to your daughter is: "As you grow up, do you want to be primarily known for your looks when there is so much more to who you are?"

It is okay for her to be mindful of her appearance, but you must be sure to affirm all the other amazing things you see in her. After all, she won't know about all the good traits that define her unless you tell her. The assurance that she is precious both inside and out is critical to giving her the self-worth she will need to sustain her through the turbulent teen years.

2. Be Careful How You Talk About Women

When you make frequent comments about the appearance of the women you know, but never mention their other strengths, your daughter will pick up on that. This is even true if all you praise in your wife is her beauty. Your girl will begin to internalize the message that you value women only for their attractiveness.

Instead, help your daughter understand that you have respect and genuine admiration for women as complete individuals, including their many other gifts and abilities.

Dads also need to be careful how they look at women. If you are prone to look a pretty woman up and down, taking in her beauty, I can assure you that your daughter will notice. A father's influence is tremendous in this area and you can be assured that she will be led to believe that

physical attractiveness is all that matters. Don't let that happen.

3. Stay Close

One message you will read over and over in this book is that you have to work hard to gain and then maintain your daughter's heart. As she changes physically and makes that sometimes-uncomfortable transition into womanhood, do not move away from her emotionally or physically. Keep hugging. Keep listening. Keep sharing quiet moments when you lay on her bed and talk with her. During this season, you can't afford to pull away. She needs you too much for you to let that happen.

> *"People's opinions of me are constantly changing. So I need to hear you say, 'I've known you forever. I've seen you at your best and your worst...and I know that you are beautiful.'"*

When you are relationally close to her, you will be able to sense when she has insecurities about her appearance. And you will be able to step in and remind her of just how lovely she is. (Be sure to ignore the eye rolls.)

MEET YOUR DAUGHTER IN THE MIDDLE

Take your daughter shopping. Give her a budget and establish a plan for what you are shopping for (summer clothes, a church dress, etc.). Look for opportunities to give

feedback on what looks nice on her, being sure to complement her at every opportunity. Be willing to coach her on issues of modesty, helping her to understand how guys view the "sexy" aspect of beauty. Use this experience to remind her that you may, on occasion, need to "veto" certain outfits when you feel like they cross a line. Above all else, remind your girl that she is lovely.

SOME THINGS TO TALK ABOUT

*Talk with your daughter about some of the wrong messages she will receive about what is beautiful.

*If you are married, share what you noticed about her mother in the early days of falling in love with her. Include her looks, but also share about what you noticed in her character and heart. Describe how those things have grown more beautiful over time.

5

Guys

At some point, your girl is going to experience a fundamental shift in how she views boys. The other gender will move from being the disgusting carriers of "cooties" to one of the basic interests of her heart. This shift happens at different times in different girls, but it is going to happen. And that's a good thing.

I can remember a season when my oldest daughter Lindsey was in the 5th grade. Whenever Lindsey was around a 9th grader from our church named Matt, a certain weirdness would surface. Sometimes she would giggle. Sometimes she would be shy. We finally theorized that Lindsey had something of a crush on Matt. When we asked Lindsey about it, she turned red, so we knew we were on to something.

Just like that, your daughter will start to develop this God-given interest in the guys around her. She will crave their

attention and she will value their opinions. Following the lead of her peers, she will probably want one to choose her to be in an exclusive relationship. Finally, she will look forward to marriage. These desires are all good, but your daughter will need help navigating the world of guys and opposite sex relationships. This is where you come in.

As a man, you have probably seen some of the humorous posts that are passed around about the "rules for dating my daughter." They provide plenty of jokes about cleaning your guns when the boy comes to pick up your girl. But if all you do is make jokes but do not offer any substantive protection and accountability for your girl, then you are failing her in a key role you have as dad.

WHY HER PERSPECTIVE OF GUYS MATTERS

You are uniquely positioned to help your daughter learn how to have healthy relationships with guys. What you do during these formative years can set the pace for how she dates and how she eventually enters marriage.

The reality is that girls learn a great deal about self-worth from their dads. They observe your marriage (or, if you are single, your relationships with the women in your life) to see how men and women should interact. If they see healthy relationships modeled by you, then they will seek those qualities in their own relationships. If you fail as a model and then fail to hold a standard of health in how guys treat her, her value system is likely to be tainted.

"I hate to admit it, but most girls are attracted to guys who are a lot like their dads."

46

Again, the foundation of this is your relationship with her. According to Linda Nielsen, a professor of psychology at Wake Forest University and an expert in father-daughter relationships, "The daughter who has a fulfilling relationship with her father is usually more trusting, more secure, and more satisfied in her romantic relationships than the daughter with a troubled or distant relationship with her dad." This holds true regardless of whether her parents are married or divorced. You have great power to both set the pace and then to help your daughter enter opposite sex relationships with healthy boundaries.

THE LIE THAT GIRLS BELIEVE ABOUT GUYS

In spite of what feminism has told our girls about independence and autonomy, she will still be tempted to believe that she has value if a boy says she has value. That's why many smart girls still crave the attention of stupid guys. It's also why they will sometimes compromise their values sexually to gain or maintain a guy's affections.

We are raising a generation of kids who are evaluating their value and identity based upon their relationship status on Facebook. The net result is that even our youngest adolescent girls feel the pressure to have a boyfriend.

Because they see the glamor and romance of their favorite stars' relationships played out in full detail, our kids have the real potential to develop an unrealistic view of what having a boyfriend or girlfriend is really like. Our younger teens who are emotionally immature, yet who see their friends pairing, up are particularly prone to this.

The message the world is giving our kids is radically different than God's Truth. Everything our kids get from the world says to "follow your heart." They hear that message in their movies, in their music, and in the very ethos of their generation. They have been fed a steady diet of that type of drivel from the Disney princess movies they watched when they were preschoolers to the top-40 music they listen to today. It is what they know by default.

> *"Dad, if my relationship with you isn't healthy, I'm likely to want an unhealthy amount of attention from a guy. That's when things go wrong."*

In contrast, Jeremiah 17:9 tells us about the questionable reliability of the heart: *"The heart is deceitful above all things and beyond cure. Who can understand it?"* According to Scripture, following one's heart can be synonymous with following a lie. It cannot be trusted and it is not always reasonable. However, because of their lack of experience and their exposure to the "trust your heart" message, our girls may not know any other way.

THE TRUTH(S) YOUR DAUGHTER DESPERATELY NEEDS TO KNOW

As her heart begins to awaken to an interest in guys and a desire to know and be known intimately, you cannot afford to check out. She needs to be constantly reminded of a few key truths. Even if she might seem to ignore your perspective, dads need to be close enough to keep giving it.

She needs to know that she is valuable apart from a guy. She is loved by God and has worth whether a guy notices

her or not. Marriage will likely be in the cards for most of our daughters, but the Bible does not make it prescriptive for every Christ-follower. That means that no man will "complete" a woman. She needs to know that.

Dads need to constantly remind their daughters that the typical teenage guy is immature and self-centered. Just as she has not yet learned to love selflessly, that cute guy she has taken an interest in probably has no comprehension at all of what true sacrificial love is. His interest in a girl is likely motivated by a selfish need for personal, or even sexual, gratification. You know this to be true because you were a teenage boy at one time. You can speak to your daughter from personal experience.

> *"I need to be reminded that guys are idiots. And dad, it's okay to confess to me that even you are an idiot sometimes."*

Finally, your daughter needs to know that one of your jobs as her father is to help her to navigate her relationships with guys. That means that it will sometimes feel like you are "all up in her business." You don't do this to be mean, but you do it because of your love for her.

The Song of Solomon contains some of the intimate words sung between lovers. It's sort of the "sexy" book in the Bible and it reads like a long love poem. On three different occasions the Scriptures say, *"Do not arouse or awaken love until it so desires."* (Song of Solomon 2:7, 3:5, and 8:4)

While Solomon's bride may have simply been telling the "daughters of Jerusalem" to let her man sleep late, I think

there is a deeper meaning here. The entire book is devoted to describing the intense love and passion that is being experienced. It is like a wild beast that, once awakened, cannot be tamed. In that context, the lovers are both describing the powerful force that they now know AND they are warning their younger siblings to not go there until they are absolutely ready to handle it. The experience is so powerful, intoxicating, and life-changing, they had better not unleash it until they are ready. Once it is awakened, it is difficult to turn off.

Regrettably, our culture encourages our girls to awaken love as soon as possible, and as often as possible. The result is that our girls are forced to grapple with the complications and challenges of giving their fully-awakened hearts away, only to see them trampled on by the carelessness of all the self-centered guys out there. They just don't have the maturity to handle the circumstances that relationships of that nature typically throw at them.

Regarding the awakening of the romantic heart in your girl, God's counsel to her is to keep it in check until she is ready to deal with it in a mature way. By talking it through and putting healthy boundaries in place, you can help your daughter to do that.

HELPING HER TO BE DIFFERENT

1. Affirm Her Interest in the Opposite Sex

Help your daughter to realize that her awakening feelings of interest and attraction to guys is, in fact, God-birthed. If you demonize or squelch those feelings, one of two things

will happen: either they will go underground and you will lose any chance to influence her, or you will foster in her a negative view of her feelings. Neither of these set the pace for a healthy marriage down the road.

Remind your daughter that your job is to help her to navigate her feelings and to help her to learn something in the process. It is also your responsibility to keep her guarded from rushing into something for which she is not yet ready. That's the value of boundaries regarding relationships. Just because you feel something, doesn't mean you have to immediately act on it.

2. Help Her Look for the Right Attributes in Guys

Your hope is that she eventually learns to identify what she is looking for in a spouse by observing the guys around her. When you see her taking an interest in a guy, ask questions like, "What do you like about him? What about him might begin to annoy you after a while?"

Another thing that dads can do for their girls is to help them ask deeper questions about the guys they are attractted to. A handsome and charming guy will always draw attention, but your girl can also learn to look a little closer at a guy by considering a few deeper issues of character:

*How does he treat others?

*Does he operate with humility?

*How does he spend his free time?

*How does he respond to authority?

*Does he speak naturally about a relationship with Christ?

While these questions can serve as a great filter for your girl to examine the guys in her world, they can also serve as a guide as she looks in the mirror. In addition to looking for the right person, dads should invest time and energy into training her to *become* the right person. Andy Stanley says it this way: "Be the person the person you are looking for is looking for."

3. Let Her Know That You Will be Involved in the Process

Share with your daughter that you are going to set some boundaries on who she dates and how and when she enters relationships. You do this because you love her. The earlier you can share this truth with her the better.

You should teach your daughter the principle of being "*equally-yoked.*" Found in 2 Corinthians 6:14, this is God's reminder to not be in a relationship with someone who doesn't share your fundamental views and faith. At our house, we established a guideline that our kids wouldn't go on a single date (even as friends to a dance) with someone who wouldn't ultimately be a potential spouse. Because, after all, your daughter has the potential to fall in love with anybody.

> *"When it comes to guys I am interested in, it matters what you say. When talking to me, be gentle, but be honest."*

Finally, at our house we have the rule that any boy who wants to date or enter a relationship with our daughters has to talk to dad first. This serves as a simple way to weed out the riffraff. (If a guy has an interest in our girl but he

won't have a conversation with dad, then he has no business hanging out with our daughter.) It also enables a dad to determine if a guy is right for his girl and to outline some key expectations for the date and/or relationship.

I get to know the boy better, asking about his personality, his hobbies, family, and his relationship with God. (Don't just ask, "Where do you go to church?" Dig deeper.) If I think he's a good guy for my daughter, I tell him expectations of how he should treat her and what a relationship is and is not going to be. (For example, "This will be one date to the dance. There will not be a second date.") If the relationship grows, we talk about physical boundaries and I assure him that we will talk about this often.

MEET YOUR DAUGHTER IN THE MIDDLE

Take her on a date and show her how she should be treated by the boys who take an interest in her. Talk about boundaries and expectations. Encourage her to welcome those moments that you ask questions about the boys she likes. Remind her that you know her and love her more than anyone, so your motivation is for her good, not to make her uncomfortable.

SOME THINGS TO TALK ABOUT

*Depending on her age, ask your daughter about what guys she has "noticed." What are the attributes that she is drawn to in the guys around her.

*Share some of what you know (and remember) about the hormonal motives of many guys. Talk about how the wrong guys value all the wrong things in a girl. Encourage her to wait until the right guy with the right motives comes along.

*Get your hands on Dennis Rainey's book, "Interviewing Your Daughter's Date." It's an easy read. Share some of the principles found in it with your girl.

6

Sex

Few fathers are particularly comfortable talking about sex with their daughters. While this is an important task of parenting, most dads are happy to relegate it to moms. And for that, our girls are probably thankful. As freaked out as you might be about discussing sexual issues with your daughter, your daughter probably feels it worse.

Unfortunately, just because something is awkward and cringe-worthy, that doesn't mean that it's not important. While moms might take the lead in talking to girls about how babies are made or a woman's monthly cycles, there are some topics where a dad's words and influence are incredibly valuable. The older your daughter gets, the more your insights will matter.

As part of your role as guard and protector of your daughter, you have a responsibility to help her to gain a healthy view of sex and its impact on her current and

future relationships. As a man, you also have a unique perspective of how most guys view sex. Your personal experiences as a teen guy (and now as a grown man) give you a certain measure of credibility and value during this season of your teen girl's life.

"Dad, do your best to normalize the conversation about sex, but don't allow it to be a trivial thing."

The challenge is having a conversation in a way that your daughter is willing to listen to your insights. While this will not be easy, it is worth doing. Even if your daughter puts her hands over her ears and screams, "LA LA LA LA" when you are talking with her, you have to persist. She does not know what she does not know. It is your job to tell her.

WHY HER VIEW OF SEX MATTERS

Teenagers have a tendency to focus only on the here and now. Because their brains are still developing, they are less able to consider the long-term consequences of their decisions.

Your daughter needs to know that her sexual activity during her pre-marriage years has the potential to negatively impact her future marriage. To put it bluntly, she needs to know that the more she connects physically with guys who are not her husband, the greater the likelihood that her marriage will end in divorce. There are plenty of sociological studies to back this up. (See our book, "The Talks," for more details.)

Too many young people today are convinced that what they do now relationally and sexually has no impact on their

futures. This could not be further from the truth. The impact is huge. South African pastor P.J. Smyth captures it this way:

"When I lived in Harare, Zimbabwe, close to our flat was the most enormous hole in the ground about the size of half a football field, and at least 40 meters deep. It was the foundation for a huge skyscraper office building. The bizarre thing was that during the pause in the work between digging the hole and starting to build, the site was totally unguarded for a few weeks. If I had the desire I could have got down into the bottom of the hole without much difficulty. Why were there no guards? Because there was nothing to protect, of course!

But let's imagine that for some reason I wanted to destroy the building. Rather than take a wrecking ball to it once it was up, I would be cunning to sneak down into the unguarded foundation, dig a couple of grave-size holes, lay some explosives that I set on a three year fuse, cover it over, climb out, walk away and relax for three years! And the beauty of it would be that they would probably never suspect that it was me!

The foundation of your marriage is your pre-marriage years. If Satan can sneak in and mess you up during those foundational years, then he is well on the way to destroying your marriage in the future."

We recognize the effects of this "pre-marriage time bomb" in the marriages we see struggling today, but the problems

are compounded for our daughters' generation. They are growing up in a culture that is more sexualized, encourages more casual relationships, and is loading them with more emotional baggage than our generation ever dreamed of.

"I confess that I'm not great at thinking about the long-term effects of my decisions."

This is why your relationship with your daughter and the coaching you offer her are so critical. Teen girls with involved fathers are far more likely to delay sexual activity compared to their peers. When a father is involved in his daughter's life, sharing openly about challenges and providing necessary accountability, the daughter is far more likely to feel valued, and therefore less likely to look for love elsewhere.

THE LIE THAT GIRLS BELIEVE ABOUT SEX

The culture is bombarding your girl with messages about sex. These messages suggest that sex should be free of boundaries, focused on self, and a reasonable part of any romantic relationship. If she does not regularly hear a contrasting message from her father, she is likely to buy what the world is selling, even if it's a horrible counterfeit to God's design.

The music, TV, and movies targeted at adolescents affirm the normalcy of emotionally and physically significant relationships, even in high school. Girls who have a regular diet of such media tend to develop a perspective that such relationships are both expected and necessary. It is during this age that the emotional connection within romantic relationships can become extremely powerful. Addition-

ally, with the cultural acceptance of same sex relationships, more and more girls are walking down that path.

At 16, when most kids begin to drive, the ante is raised. Freed from the restrictions of parents and the limitations of group activities, couples who are "Facebook official" will likely see intimate kissing, sexual touching, oral sex, and even intercourse as normal, reasonable dimensions of their relationship.

Your little girl who never dreamed of letting a guy take advantage of her will find herself tempted to give in sexually in ways that she never dreamed of just a few years before. Her world tells her that this is completely normal. As long as she consents and uses protection, it is all okay. She desperately needs to hear an alternative narrative from her father.

THE TRUTH YOUR DAUGHTER DESPERATELY NEEDS TO KNOW

While you can and should speak to her about God's design of saving sexual behavior (not just sexual intercourse) for marriage, you can best do this by giving her a chemistry lesson. Specifically, your daughter needs to know about a powerful little chemical called oxytocin. This "drug" has the potential to influence her more than alcohol, marijuana, and all other illegal substances combined.

Oxytocin is known in scientific circles as "the bonding chemical." It is secreted in both men and women, helping to create meaningful bonds and attachments to others. It also gives one a sense of euphoria in the deepest places of

the mind and body. As you might expect, oxytocin is most powerfully generated in times of sexual intimacy. Unfortunately, oxytocin doesn't have a brain. It doesn't know if who you are connecting to is someone worth connecting to.

Oxytocin is one of the reasons that sex makes people so stupid. Your daughter needs to know that sexual activity outside of marriage has the potential to make you crazy in love with a complete bozo. It's why two young people, who seem to have nothing in common, and who are rarely seen getting along very well, can't seem to break up. They are confusing lust with love and oxytocin is effectively serving as the fuel that's powering their foolishness. Sexual intimacy has incredible power to mask relationship flaws.

"Girls desperately want to be loved, and girls will sometimes do stupid things to feel loved."

God created oxytocin to work in marriage. It generates powerful bonds and keeps two people crazy in love with one another. It does just the opposite in teen relationships. It might keep a couple running back to one another, but it undermines the substantive parts of the relationship that are necessary to help it last long-term.

Even in the Bible's original language, God made an important distinction between sex before marriage and sex in marriage. The English language has one main word for sex: it's sex. That word is used to describe a great big variety of behaviors and activities.

But in the original Hebrew of the Old Testament, God was careful to show us extreme contrasts in the different types of sex. One word for sex, *yada*, is used to describe sex

within a covenant marriage. It's the word used to describe the perfect and secure intimacy that Adam and Eve experienced: *"Now Adam had sexual relations with his wife, Eve, and she became pregnant."* (Genesis 4:1) The word for sex here implies "to know." It is an extreme level of intimacy reserved for marriage.

In contrast, there are plenty of places in the Bible where God is describing the sexual act, but it's not happening how He designed it, in the context of marriage. In those instances, the Bible will usually use the word *shakab*. It implies more of a "spilling of seed." It is a meaningless physical act, not rooted in anything of substance.

Dannah Gresh puts it this way: "Some sex is God's sex. It's *yada*. Some sex is a mere counterfeit. It's *shakab*. Same plumbing, but a totally different thing."

God wants us to deny ourselves the shallow, selfish experience of *shakab* so we can best experience the intimate knowing found in *yada*. He wants us to fully enjoy His gift of sex, free of all the baggage that most people pick up as they navigate their teen and young adult years. That's why He tells us to wait.

> *"Dad, if I am in a romantic relationship, you're going to have to regularly check in on me and my boyfriend. We need some accountability regarding the physical part of our relationship."*

HELPING HER TO BE DIFFERENT

1. Teach Her That Her Sexuality is Precious and Worth Guarding.

You can use the age-old arguments for why she should save sex for marriage – pregnancy and STDs – but those are not the best reasons to wait. In fact, if those are the main things she hears from you, then you're making a pretty weak argument. Today's teenager can zip into CVS and spend $1.50 on a simple and occasionally reliable solution to those problems. You need to stress something grander.

Something as beautiful and holy and fulfilling as "yada" shouldn't be treated casually like "shakab." Her God-given sexuality is a precious thing that has incredible potential to create joy and bring intimacy to her marriage one day. It is worth protecting. Saving it for marriage is a key part of building strength into what will eventually be her most important human relationship.

2. Remind Her of the Reality of Sexual Temptation

For most of our kids, the desire for sexual activity will show up in the context of a romantic relationship. Your daughter may make a commitment to sexual purity, but once she gets emotionally and relationally connected to a guy she likes, sexual temptation is probably just around the corner. We call that season of life between late adolescence and marriage "the great tribulation," where young adults are wired for sex but are convicted to put it off until later.

> *"Go into detail about the emotional and spiritual messiness of pre-marital sexual relationships. I don't fully get that, so you have to keep explaining it to me."*

This is a spiritual battle. The very thing that Satan is using as a temptation is incredibly attractive in the moment. After all, we don't need to be convinced to flee from something that is clearly dangerous, like a swarm of killer

bees or a grizzly bear. In the case of sexual activity, you must help your daughter to see that what seems so good will actually be a source of pain and grief. She shouldn't be surprised when it happens, and she must be prepared to deal with it when it does.

3. Equip Her with Some "Scripts" for When Temptation Occurs

One key thing you can do is to prepare your daughter for what she can do and say when she finds herself in an uncomfortable situation. She might not be able to predict what she might encounter out there, but you can.

Give her some scenarios of what she might encounter at school, on a date, or at a party. Then, help her create a clear plan of what to do in each case. The key is that you need to talk about fleeing sexual temptation long before your daughter is walking out the door with her prom date. Practice this stuff early, even if it is awkward. Too many of our daughters are ill prepared for what they face because no one has helped them to get ready.

MEET YOUR DAUGHTER IN THE MIDDLE

Everybody is talking about sex. Movies, music, friends, etc. are all sources of information and perspective about human sexuality. Sadly, most dads and daughters are not having these conversations. Find some time to be alone in the car with your girl, even if it's just a short drive to school or a friend's house. (Shoulder to shoulder is better than face to face for this conversation.) Let her know that you desperately want to be a "safe place" she can talk about her

perspectives of sex. She can ask you questions about boys or about feelings. Tell her that you take very seriously your job of helping her to avoid foolish or emotionally painful choices. Remind her that you do this because you love her.

SOME THINGS TO TALK ABOUT

*Ask her about what she hears her friends (and others) at her school talking about sex. How diverse are their perspectives? Who is being particularly foolish?

*As much as you feel comfortable, share some of the regrets that you have from any poor sexual or relational decisions made during your pre-marriage years.

*At every chance you have, try to communicate a positive view of sex to your daughter. God created it to be a blessing, but with clear parameters: in a heterosexual covenant marriage.

7

Pornography

It is likely that the minute you saw the title of this chapter, you had an emotional response. As a man, you likely have had some experience with porn. If you haven't ever looked at it or been exposed to it, then God bless you. You're like a unicorn: a strange creature that the rest of us don't believe actually exists.

For the rest of us, our exposure to porn is probably varied. Maybe you saw some stuff early in your teen years but it never really took hold in your life. Perhaps it was a significant struggle back in those days. But if statistics are accurate, a good number of dads reading these words are still struggling. You're still looking at porn on a regular basis.

Let's agree that porn has traditionally been more of a guy problem. For generations, young men have been drawn to sexually explicit images. While you can probably remember

early exposure to Playboy or Penthouse, what our kids have available to them via online content has changed absolutely everything. And while you had to work really hard to find porn when you were a teenager, most of our kids are carrying what are essentially "porn delivery devices" in their pockets.

WHY HER OPINION OF PORN MATTERS

Dr. Chap Clark of the Fuller Youth Institute says that 60% of teen boys in America are addicted to porn. He defined "addicted" as 3 visits per week to a porn site at one hour per visit. The statistics on porn use among teenage girls are almost as bad. One study determined that more than a third of teenage girls reported that they had watched porn recently.

This early exposure to graphic sexual content is significantly affecting our kids. Parents have to take it seriously. If you knew that 60% of the teenagers in your community were regularly using meth or heroin, you would be aggressively militant in your attempt to help your kids stay clean. You would talk about it. Often.

We must take the porn issue just as seriously. Because habitual porn use gives a dopamine rush, brain pathways are established and an addiction is fostered. Scientists say that it is just as significant and powerful as any drug addiction. It is literally re-shaping the users' brains.

Online pornography is also giving an entire generation a lousy education about sex. The work we have done with young newlywed couples has convinced us that there is some bad news for the smartphone generation. Their collective perspective on what sex is and what God meant

for it to be has been significantly altered.

If your daughter has a struggle with porn, she will likely carry that problem into marriage. We interact with many newlyweds who are convinced that their porn problems will go away once they have a healthy outlet for their sexual desires within the context of marriage. Rarely does it happen that easily.

The bottom line is that potential for private, sexual sin is very high among our daughters' generation. We must get comfortable talking about it. We have to tell our girls (and, of course, our boys) that porn has the power to negatively impact their lives. We must teach them some practical steps to face the temptation that they will encounter on a daily basis, perhaps for the rest of their lives. And with most kids seeing porn for the first time in elementary school, it is a conversation that we need to have sooner rather than later.

THE LIES THAT GIRLS BELIEVE ABOUT PORN

To look at porn, our fathers' generation had to head to a seedy adult theater in a bad part of town. Thanks to Hugh Hefner, our generation experienced a shift in the "normalization" of explicit content. Because of the articles (yeah, right) porn became mainstream and our culture came to accept it as a normal, if not healthy, reality.

Fast forward to our daughters' generation. Exposure to (and the use of) porn has become the norm in her culture and among her peers. If something can be easily accessed via a smartphone or a home computer, then it must be

okay. As I heard one teenager recently say, "Everyone looks at it, so it must not be a big deal."

"Dad, porn use is more common for girls than you would ever know."

Unfortunately, all this early exposure to porn is impacting how teenagers discover and experiment with their own sexuality. Even what boys expect from girls has dramatically changed. In her groundbreaking book, "Girls and Sex," author Peggy Orenstein writes that for many girls, oral sex is the new first base. She shares how many young women feel obligated to gratify the sexual requests of guys who have come to see porn as the standard for sexual behavior.

Even the issue of self-image comes into play. If your girl is exposed to enough porn, her perception of what is normal regarding her physical appearance will inevitably be impacted. If she sees enough surgically enhanced bodies and bleached blonde hair, she may come to think that her "normal" body doesn't measure up. At a time when insecurity runs rampant in the teen girl psyche, this is pressure she doesn't need.

THE TRUTH YOUR DAUGHTER DESPERATELY NEEDS TO KNOW

An entire generation is learning about sex from looking at online pornography. And they are getting a terrible education. Simply put, watching porn to learn about sex is sort of like playing Nintendo Mario Cart to learn how to drive. It's just not helpful. It's so far removed from reality

that it hurts far worse than it helps.

"Girls are just as curious about sex as boys are. Unfortunately, that might lead me to some pretty dark places online."

Your girl needs to know that if she has questions about sex or boys, she can ask you or your wife. Obviously, she is more likely to go to her mom, but there are some conversations that dad needs to step into, as well. The porn conversation is one of those.

Your daughter needs to be reminded that the entire dynamic of sex displayed in the typical porn video is a lie. Sex in porn is usually guy-focused and the girl is just a tool to meet his desires. If she believes that (or the guy she dates believes that) they are missing out on the fundamental role that sex has in the marriage relationship. It's about oneness, intimacy, AND pleasure. It's not about getting what you want but about generously giving to your spouse. Porn undermines all of that. That's why it is so critical that we avoid it.

Long before the modern pornography industry introduced the possibility of sexual sin that can be experienced in private, God knew it would be a reality. Whether it's our thought life or the deliberate seeking out of explicit images and videos, we are prone to foolish behavior. Given how easy it is to struggle with this, God gives a very simple prescription for those who want to walk in victory.

In I Corinthians 6:18, Paul writes, *"Flee from sexual immorality. All other sins a person commits are outside the body, but whoever sins sexually, sins against their own body."* This word speaks to both the seriousness of

sexual sin and the simple (though not always easy) solution.

In no uncertain terms, we need to tell our kids that if they ever encounter even a hint of sexually explicit content, they need to flee. Run. Step away from the computer or device. Remove themselves immediately from the situation. The longer they flirt with it, the harder it will be to disengage.

This is important because no other behavior operates quite like a "slippery slope" more than sexual sin. The more porn you see, the more you want to look. Typically, the content becomes increasingly explicit as you go deeper down the rabbit hole. While some things might seem harmless, they have the high likelihood of leading to more destructive – and habit forming – content. That's why the best solution is to flee.

HELPING HER TO BE DIFFERENT

Talking about fleeing sexual sin and actually doing it are entirely different things. That's why parents (and particularly dads) have to equip their girls with the skills they will need to guard their hearts and minds from all the junk they will encounter online. Here are a few places to start helping them.

1. Teach Her to Bounce Her Eyes

A simple skill that every person needs to learn is the "eye bounce." Sure, we will notice sexual images all around us, but we can choose to immediately look away. First mentioned in his book "Every Man's Battle," Stephen Arterburn suggests that a lot can happen in that split-second when we first notice an image that is sexual in nature. Before a look or a thought takes hold in our minds,

we can quickly move on to something else. It's like a quick conversation with yourself that says, "That's not for me."

"As you talk about this stuff, don't communicate that you don't trust me. But still, empower me with the tools I need to navigate this junk."

It's sort of like what Job declared in Job 31:1. His commitment was simple: *"I made a covenant with my eyes not to look lustfully at a young woman."* If this faithful man had to make a commitment to protect his eyes, then every one of us would be wise to do likewise. Encourage your daughter to be diligent in this, praying that God would do in her what she is likely unable to do on her own. If and when she sees something online, she can ask God for the strength to shut it down immediately.

2. Lead Her to Pray for Those in the Porn Industry

A second discipline for our kids who will be susceptible to lust and temptation is to teach them to pray for those who are caught up in the sex trade. This includes people who are caught in the porn industry. According to most of the people who have gotten out of porn, the whole environment is one rampant with abuse, drug use, and exploitation. These people are trapped in a world that is doing significant damage to their hearts and souls. They deserve our mercy and our prayers. Plus, as a friend once said, it is really hard to lust after someone for whom I am praying.

There are many great organizations who are working to help these people to choose a different life. Perhaps exploring the articles and resources that these ministries offer will give your daughter new insight into how she can

pray. *XXX Church* and *Fight The New Drug* are both good places to start. Of course, be careful not to expose your daughter to so much content that her curiosity kicks in and takes her places she doesn't need to go. Pray for wisdom.

3. Put Parameters on Your Family's Technology

A final recommendation we make to every parent is that we put parameters on the computers and smartphones in our homes. If we have children or teens and our devices do not have some form of filter or blocking software, we are asking for trouble. I will go one step further and call it foolish. You may have complete trust in your kids and you may want them to learn to make wise decisions on their own. Fine. But when you took your preschooler to the pool, you gave her clear instructions and expectations for her safety, but you also made her wear a life preserver. Both are important.

> *"You can put some software on my smartphone, but I still need you to talk about this, even if it's awkward."*

Unfortunately, the reality is that there is no magic switch you can throw to block all the explicit content that can enter your home via your devices. Even Instagram (probably your daughter's go-to social networking app) contains porn. If you look hard enough, you can find it everywhere. That's why you have to keep talking about it. It's not going away any time soon.

MEET YOUR DAUGHTER IN THE MIDDLE

Talk about the temptation to look at sexually explicit content and discuss the need for accountability and safeguards in your home. Do some research together on some of the filtering and accountability tools available on the market today and then decide on one that will work for your family. (We recommend tools such as Circle and Covenant Eyes) Decide on what parameters you will set for her and let her give input into how you will remain accountable, as well. Agree that this is a struggle for every person in your family.

SOME THINGS TO TALK ABOUT

*As you feel comfortable, share your struggles with porn and the negative impact it has had on your life.

*Assume that the boys she dates will have had at least some exposure to porn. Talk about the impact that will have on their relationship. Help her to establish personal boundaries and encourage her to share them with anyone she dates.

*Talk a whole lot about the grace of God for our sin, particularly the sexual sin that gives so many people shame. If she has looked at porn in the past, remind her that, because of the cross, God loves us and restores us completely.

8

Security

Over the past year or so, numerous stories have surfaced of women who have been taken advantage of by men in positions of power. Starting with movie producer Harvey Weinstein, hundreds of men have been brought into account for their (alleged) past sexual aggressions and abuses. This is a very good thing. It's as if our entire culture has finally declared that we are not going to tolerate men behaving badly.

This sort of behavior is more common than most of us could ever imagine. It doesn't just happen in Hollywood. You have likely seen #MeToo or #NoMore written by someone you know and love. If you're like me, it has been multiple someones. These simple hashtags are giving a voice to the millions of women (and men) who have experienced some form of unwanted sexual activity.

The thought of someone taking advantage of your daughter

either by violence or sexual aggression is probably enough to make your blood boil. But while your little girl was easy to protect when she was safely under the guard of your home, she's in the process of growing up and moving on. You won't always be there to shield her from danger. That's why talking with your daughter and preparing her for what might happen is one of your biggest roles as dad.

"There were several years I was being raised by a single mom. When she remarried, I can't tell you how secure it felt to once again live under a father's care and security."

WHY YOUR PROTECTION MATTERS

Sex is hard enough to talk to your daughter about, much less having to deal with the horrifying possibility that someone could attempt to bring her harm. If you have done a sub-par job of discussing sex and sexual boundaries with your daughter, it is likely that you are also living in a fog of denial about the real possibility of sexual abuse. Because of your discomfort and reluctance to talk, your daughter may be vulnerable.

The statistics are hard to quantify (because so much abuse goes unreported), but one study suggests that one out of every three women will be a victim of either sexual assault or domestic violence at some point in their lives. The hope is that recent public discourse is reversing those trends. No longer are victims of abuse shamed into silence, afraid of the repercussions of disclosure.

While we have all heard the stories of assault in the workplace that make headlines, you should be just as concerned

about the potentially aggressive actions of the young men that your girl will date. Unfortunately, a vulnerable girl alone with a boy who has less-than-noble intentions can lead to a situation with significant emotional (and even physical) casualties.

> *"My best intentions of sexual purity may easily go out the window when I'm alone with my boyfriend. I hate to admit it, but it's true."*

It would be great to be able to give every young man the benefit of the doubt. After all, most men don't have evil intentions. But as long as men are stronger than women (and boys are stronger than girls), there will always be some risk of your daughter getting taken advantage of. That's why you have to be diligent.

THE LIE THAT GIRLS BELIEVE ABOUT THEIR SAFETY

It's a contrary world that our girls live in. On one hand, the entertainment elite has decried sexual aggression and demonized any man who treats a woman as a toy to be played with. This is a very good thing. But on the other hand, the same people recently celebrated the life and work of Hugh Hefner, the founder of Playboy. Make no mistake: this is the man who brought porn into the mainstream and who inadvertently got the ball rolling for an entire generation of young men to embrace a distorted view of sex.

Add to that the mixed message that our girls are getting regarding their sexuality. They are told that they can be just as sexual as guys can be. In some ways, this is true and

long overdue. Unfortunately, the "sexual empowerment" message has not helped our teen girls. It fosters behaviors that ultimately leave them wounded and hurt.

Through all this, our girls can wrongly believe the lie that they are bulletproof. They don't need the oversight of anyone, certainly not their fathers. They can fearlessly believe that, while bad things happen to other people, there is no way something bad would ever happen to them.

Our culture has made them overly confident, while not fully preparing them to guard and protect their hearts, minds, and bodies.

THE TRUTH YOUR DAUGHTER DESPERATELY NEEDS TO KNOW

As your daughter grows up and begins to daily enter a world where she is vulnerable, she needs to know that you are there to protect and take care of her. While you might not always be with her physically, you will be her advocate and provide whatever oversight you are able to give.

> *"I constantly go back and forth between feeling entirely safe and feeling entirely vulnerable. Dad, there's a part of me that knows I will always want you to protect me."*

Dads, your girl may push away from you, but she is still looking to you for protection. If she feels unsafe or alone, know that any step you take to intervene and be present will give her security in her mind and connection with your heart.

Along her life's journey, if she encounters some form of abuse or aggression, she must be confident that she can count on you to be in her corner. That includes believing in her and even reporting the abuser to the appropriate authorities.

Your girl also needs to know that you are not always going to be present with her. She's going to have to learn some skills to protect herself. A part of your equipping should be to help her to steer clear of circumstances where she might be vulnerable. She needs to learn how to look for "red flags" in the context of relationships, in social situations, and even in the workplace. There's a great example of this in God's word....

1 Samuel 13 tells the tragic story of David's son Amnon and his sick obsession with his sister Tamar. It serves as a cautionary tale and a textbook case of someone who missed all the warning signs. Amnon desperately wanted to have sex with Tamar, so at the suggestion of one of his advisors, he devised a plan to get her alone. He pretended to be sick and then asked his father David to send Tamar to care for him and make him some homemade bread.

The first person to miss a red flag was David, Tamar's father. Whether he was too busy to notice Amnon's obsession or he was simply naïve, we do not know. What we do know is that David sent his daughter into a very hazardous situation. (There's a lesson for every dad reading this.)

Tamar went to Amnon's room and made bread right there in his presence. She did just as he requested, but Amnon wouldn't eat it. He suddenly acted like he wasn't interested. There's the second red flag. He said one thing and did another. You must train your daughter to become very

alert when she finds herself in a situation when a guy says one thing but then changes his mind.

The third red flag that Tamar should have noticed was when Amnon sent everyone else out of his room, leaving her alone with him. This is clearly significant. A good rule to enforce with your daughter is that she should not be alone in any isolated place with a guy, even if he has been trustworthy in the past. Our kids may have the best of intentions, but the potential for temptation is great.

A final red flag came when Amnon asked Tamar to sit on his bed and feed him. This was the same guy who just a few minutes ago said he wasn't hungry. In those moments when your daughter senses that something isn't right, it is probably because something isn't right. That troubling sense is most likely the Holy Spirit of God warning her to flee.

In Tamar's case, she could have seen some of the red flags, expressed a measure of discomfort with the whole situation, and bolted for the door. Because she didn't, she suffered a tragic sexual assault at the hands of someone she trusted.

HELPING HER TO BE DIFFERENT

1. Empower Your Daughter

The sooner parents can give their girls a voice against any form of sexual abuse, the better. A dad must help his daughter to understand that there is power in her voice and that no one can take that power away from her. Remind her that she can always say "NO" or "STOP" if she feels uncomfortable with a guy. If that is not sufficient, she

may need to fight back.

"If a guy tried something with me and I wasn't prepared for it, I could easily see myself freezing up in fear or shock."

Regarding this issue, the most powerful tools you can give your daughter are preparation, clear boundaries, and personal power. There is a lifetime of these lessons to teach, often practiced in the most risky of situations. Most importantly, your girl needs to know that you love her and that you will always believe her and support her in any case of sexual abuse.

2. Train Her to Be a "Hard Target"

If you watch a television show about African wildlife on a nature channel, you will probably get a quick lesson about predators and prey. A hungry lion will always pick out the most weak and frail animal from within a herd to single out for his lunch. Guys looking to take advantage of a girl will do the same. That's why your daughter has to be cautious.

Your girl definitely needs to know about date rape drugs. While the most popular one is Rohypnol (Roofies), other drugs commonly used include GHB, Ketamine, and even Ambien. They need to know how these are used and that even charming and good-looking young men will try to slip them into their drinks at parties. One specific lesson to teach your girl: "At a party, do not EVER take a drink that someone gives you. Ever."

Beyond the drugs that are used by men to take advantage of women, we must coach our girls that recreational drugs and alcohol can quickly make them targets of sexual abuse.

A few headline-grabbing trials in recent days have showed us that foolish and energetic young men have the real potential to take advantage of young women who are not fully sober. That's why drinking in social situations can be so dangerous.

3. Watch For Signs That Something has Happened

Dads, throughout your daughter's developmental years, you should constantly be on the lookout for significant changes in her behavior that might suggest something has happened to her. Granted, girls can be on a roller coaster of emotions until they reach their twenties, but witnessing a dramatic change in behavior should encourage you to dig a little deeper. While it may just be teenager stuff, there may be a need to probe a little bit deeper. Ask questions like:

· Has anything happened between you and _____?

· Sometimes a person might make you feel uncomfortable or even hurt you, and then warn you that you can't tell anyone. Know that any person who says that cannot be trusted. Has that ever happened to you?

· I'm here to help you and keep you safe. If you don't feel safe with someone, it is always okay for you to tell me about it.

The bottom line is that you would love to launch your girl into adulthood free of any fear of anyone ever harming her physically or sexually. But statistically, there's a good chance that she will one day be a victim in some way. Training her to be prepared might not help her to avoid it completely, but it will empower her to respond.

MEET YOUR DAUGHTER IN THE MIDDLE

Scan the internet for news stories about men taking advantage of women. There are plenty of them to browse through. While an assault is never the woman's fault, talk about ways that the women might have placed themselves at risk. Discuss some specific personal boundaries that your daughter might choose to enforce for herself on dates and even in the workplace to stay guarded.

SOME THINGS TO TALK ABOUT

* Hopefully, your daughter is up to date with current events and knows that she should not tolerate any form of unwanted sexual aggression. If not, have a conversation about that.

*Ask your daughter if she knows anyone who has been taken advantage of or even assaulted by a guy in some way.

*Remind her of the importance of staying sober and alert...and of making sure she is there to watch out for her peers who might not be.

9

God

Before you know it, a day will arrive in the life of your daughter that you probably have some mixed feelings about. She will leave home and begin her life beyond your supervision and oversight. During that new season, she's not going to have you around to lead her or to tell her what to do or when to be home. How will she ever survive without you?

It depends. How she gets along as she transitions to independent adulthood depends on a few things. Have you effectively prepared her for the challenges she will face? Have you equipped her to manage friendships and romantic relationships with maturity? Have you given her confidence in herself and the educational and real world opportunities to succeed in the path she has chosen? Have you instilled in her the character she will need to make wise choices in the face of the foolishness of others?

All of these things matter, but one thing matters more than all of them combined. Specifically, she needs to know God in a real and personal way. Not know about God, but know Him personally.

Your daughter might be highly successful in every area of her life, but if she isn't connected to God, none of it ultimately matters. She will likely spend her days climbing the ladder of success, only to reach the top to discover that it's leaning against the wrong wall. She needs the direction, purpose, and peace that can only come through staying connected to her Creator.

WHY HER RELATIONSHIP WITH GOD MATTERS

Your job of raising and teaching and leading your daughter will soon be over. You will always have a place in her life, but the heavy lifting is coming to a close. That's why your greatest goal during these years of influence should be to help your daughter to walk with the One who will always be there for her.

> *"Lots of parents stay the mediator between God and their kids. Dad, I need you to teach me to walk personally with God....to find Him."*

It's not like God is taking over for you. He's always been there, wanting to lead and guide her towards an awesome and meaningful life. It's just that it is very easy for a child, or even a teenager, to allow her parents to take the place of God in her life. Why listen for the voice of God when she is required to listen to mom and dad?

Once she leaves home, she will need God's guidance more than ever before. And in a world where some studies suggest that more than half of all Christian young people abandon their faith in college, the stakes have never been higher. She is going to encounter a world of moral relativism that is often antagonistic towards people with an unwavering trust in God.

If your girl has experience walking in a love relationship with God, she will have already been able to *"taste and see that the Lord is good."* She will have already learned that finding her place in God's big story is the most important thing she can do. She will know that a life rooted in and submitted to Jesus will be a life of purpose. Successfully taught, these things will stay with her long after she moves out of your home.

THE LIES THAT GIRLS BELIEVE ABOUT GOD

Over the past few years, strange shifts have happened on the American college campus. Where you used to find great diversity of thought and generous freedom to debate varying worldviews, now you find more close-mindedness than ever before. Even traditional Christian values can be seen as hate-speech.

As a result, many young women (and men) from your daughter's generation are landing at one of three places regarding the place that God will play in their lives:

The first one concludes that God is irrelevant. He is old-fashioned and no longer has a meaningful place in modern society. Given what we know about people and science and

love, it is apparent that the "way of life" found in the Bible no longer has a place. Jesus was a nice guy, but only the parts that make us feel good about ourselves and our life choices. It is entirely reasonable not to believe in God.

> *"I see few examples of people who are truly committed to Jesus. The result is that I'm not regularly convinced that it's worth it."*

The second conclusion is that God is just one part of the American dream. You see this world-view embraced by many well-intentioned people in the Bible belt. Your daughter will encounter this view in many of her Christian peers on the college campus. They are nice people that will follow Jesus as long as following Jesus guarantees a good career, a successful husband, two kids, and a nice house in the suburbs.

A final conclusion is that God is far away and doesn't want to be disturbed. Many young people who believe in God assume that He is very busy. They may seek Him out when they are facing a big decision, but choose to keep Him at arm's length in their daily lives. They miss out on the very relationship of love and intimacy that God has invited each of us into through Jesus.

THE TRUTH YOUR DAUGHTER DESPERATELY NEEDS TO KNOW

Perhaps the most important truth you can teach your daughter is that God is living, active, and relevant to her life today. He has a plan for her and is offering her the invitation to join Him in the big story of redemption He is

telling in the world. While that starts when she submits to God's plan of salvation through faith in Jesus, it doesn't stop there. Through every stage of life, she needs to know that God is with her to lead her and guide her.

"I need you to take my burdens seriously and to teach me how to turn to God in the midst of the challenges I am facing."

Even in those times when she gets it wrong, God is there for her, offering His love and grace. He doesn't freak out when she sins or fails or chooses the wrong path. While the enemy of our God might trick her into thinking that God is losing patience with her, He never ever does. He is constantly pursuing her, wanting to be close to her. There is nothing she can do to make God love her any more or any less. When she blows it, she can always run to Him.

As a father, you can teach your daughter that God has a voice and that listening to Him is critical. When seeking direction for life or when confronted with temptation, God is there to lead her. Spending time talking with God and feeding on Scripture will put your daughter in a position to know His will and to hear His voice. Those who know God's Word best hear His voice the clearest.

The key place that your daughter will learn about the importance of walking with God is from watching her parents. And even though you don't share her gender, some studies suggest that she will learn this best by watching you, her father. Your example speaks far more loudly than any lecture you might give her.

This is illustrated perfectly in what might be the most powerful parenting passage in the Bible. In Exodus 33:8-

11, we find the Israelites wandering in the desert after their deliverance from Egypt. God instructed Moses to create a "tent of meeting" that would serve as the unique place where God would speak with him.

> *And whenever Moses went out to the tent, all the people rose and stood at the entrances to their tents, watching Moses until he entered the tent. As Moses went into the tent, the pillar of cloud would come down and stay at the entrance, while the Lord spoke with Moses. Whenever the people saw the pillar of cloud standing at the entrance to the tent, they all stood and worshiped, each at the entrance to their tent. The Lord would speak to Moses face to face, as one speaks to a friend. Then Moses would return to the camp, but his young aide Joshua son of Nun did not leave the tent.*

The parenting principle is tucked right there at the very end. Scripture says that Joshua, Moses' young apprentice, would not leave the tent after Moses and God shared their time there. The implication is that Joshua saw what Moses had with God – how it impacted his life and gave him direction and purpose – and wanted what Moses had. It is as if he would linger there in the tent saying, "God, can you speak to me like you speak to Moses?"

> *"Dad, you're going to have to lead by example. Not to put any pressure on you, but I'm always paying attention to what you value and how you spend your time."*

The point is that those who are coming behind you will learn how to walk with God by watching you walk with

God. If you naturally and regularly demonstrate a meaningful, joyful, rich life that is rooted in your relationship with Jesus, your daughter will likely want what you have. If, on the other hand, you occasionally tip your hat to God on Sunday mornings, but don't live your life in pursuit of Him, your daughter will notice. She will learn that everything else in life is more important than the place that God plays in one's life. God will be simply an afterthought.

HELPING HER TO BE DIFFERENT

All of this begs a few questions for personal reflection: What does your daughter see in you? Are you modeling a good example of what it looks like to walk with God? What is she learning about the vital importance of staying close to God from watching your life? If you're not sure of what you are showing her and teaching her, there are a few places you can start...

1. Re-prioritize Your Relationship with God

If you would admit that your heart isn't turned towards the things of God right now, maybe it's time to start. And if you don't feel all that motivated, you could begin by asking God to supernaturally put that motivation into your heart and mind. Trust me, that's a prayer that God wants to answer "yes" to. If you ask Him for passion for Him, He will begin to give it to you.

As you walk in a daily relationship with God and He becomes increasingly more important to you, it is likely that you will come to talk openly about Him. Let your daughter hear you. If God and His presence and activity are a regular part of your life, it will spill out of you. You

don't have to force it. You just have to share what God is teaching you and where you see Him at work. Ultimately, she will learn how to walk with God by watching you.

2. Parent Like Jesus

Every father has flaws and will let their kids down in some ways. You're not going to be perfect. But there is a big difference between a dad who occasionally drops the ball and one who consistently runs the wrong way. We speak to far too many young women who have a hard time seeing God as a loving father because of the legalistic, distant, and hard-to-please natures of their earthly fathers.

This bears repeating: much of what your daughter will learn about the nature of God will come by interacting with you. If you consistently love her, lead her, and forgive her like God does, she will long to be close to you. As she gets older and discovers more and more what God is like (as imperfectly modeled by you), she will long to be close to Him. You're setting the pace and the stakes are very high in terms of "how" you parent.

3. Help Her to Value God's Perspective

As your daughter grows up and begins to make more significant life decisions, she will need a process to determine God's will for her life.

> *"I would LOVE it if you would occasionally ask me, 'How can I pray for you?'"*

While there are no secret formulas, you can consistently remind her that God does have an opinion on what she does, what she studies, the career she pursues, the guys she

dates (and marries), and every other big and small part of her life.

The hard part of this is that, in most cases, God's calling and standards will run contrary to the value system of the world and many of her peers. God calls us not to fit Him into our lives but to lay down our lives in pursuit of Him. While this call to radical surrender and discipleship is never easy, it is the key to a life of meaning and purpose.

Dad, you can join the masses of people who are telling your daughter to follow her heart and to do what she wants with her life. Or, you can teach her to seek something better: a powerful love relationship with the One who made her and who has dreamed big dreams for her since the beginning of time. Choose wisely.

MEET YOUR DAUGHTER IN THE MIDDLE

Buy a journal for your daughter and make sure she has a modern translation of the Bible. (We recommend the NIV or NLT.) Sit down with her and teach her a simple way to read the Bible that will connect her with God and move her towards life-change. Simply read a passage (start with a parable of Jesus) and ask three simple questions: "What? (What does it say?) So what? (What does it mean?) Now what? (What specifically do I need to do in response to it?)

Encourage her to write out her responses to those three questions. Have her jot down some personal prayer requests and then teach her to talk to God about those things and the insights she gets from her reading. Beyond

having a time to connect with God like this, teach your daughter that God is always close to her, so she can talk to Him at any time.

SOME THINGS TO TALK ABOUT

*Tell her about a time when you felt very close to God. What were you doing to facilitate that? What did that season of life feel like?

*Brainstorm together a way that the two of you might hold each other accountable in your relationships with God. Commit to texting each other prayer requests on a regular basis.

10

The Middle

Hopefully you and your daughter have worked your way through this book and have had some meaningful conversations along the way. Now that you have finally reached "the middle," we wanted to challenge you with one final thing and then lead you to a commitment.

Experts in educational psychology assert that you best remember the first and last things you hear. So if the first thing you read in this book is that your daughter desperately needs your presence and leadership in her life, then this last thing is equally as important.

The last thing we want to leave you with is something we have hinted at several times over the past 100 pages. But just in case you missed it, we wanted to be perfectly clear:

Your daughter needs to know that your love for her is unconditional.

Now, we know what you're thinking. You've got this one nailed down. Your daughter totally knows that you love her unconditionally, right?

But does she really?

Just because you feel it and have maybe even said it, your daughter may not fully believe it. What we heard from many of the young women we talked to was that dad had good intentions, but his daily leadership and interactions with her communicated that she had to perform or measure up to a certain standard to be fully loved.

If they failed or were a disappointment in some way, many of these girls felt like their dads' love was withheld or removed. With tears in their eyes, they communicated that dad was more of a taskmaster who was never satisfied than a benevolent father who loves consistently.

That is why you have to be intentional to regularly communicate your unconditional love for your daughter. Her insecure female heart doesn't always believe she is loveable, especially during these awkward years of adolescence. That's why you have to tell her. Double down on this truth regularly.

The need for her to experience your love is perhaps greatest when she screws up in some way. During those times, while there may be a need for discipline or punishment, you need to offer an abundance of grace.

As Christ described in the parable of the prodigal son, dads should always be ready to offer second chances. If your family values are more marked by right and wrong than they are by repentance and restoration, then you are missing the point. Because the primary message of the

gospel is forgiveness, not rules, there is great value in making sure that your daughter clearly knows that there is nothing that she can ever do that will make you stop loving her. May God help you to communicate that to her!

Never stop pursuing her heart.

The emotional connection between a father and daughter is a precious and valuable thing. You have to work at capturing her heart and then, once you have it, you have to work at maintaining it. Just like in our relationship with our heavenly Father, love is a far better motivator than fear of wrath. Both have their place, but love is far more powerful.

So, how do you know if you have your daughter's heart? I once heard it explained this way:

Imagine a circumstance where your daughter is out with friends on a Friday night and is being tempted to participate in some immoral or illegal activity: drinking alcohol, for example. At that critical moment of decision, one of two possible thoughts will go through her mind:

"If my dad finds out about this, he will kill me."

Or the other possibility:

"If my dad finds out about this, it will kill him."

Do you notice the subtle difference? The first thought shows that your daughter is most worried about a possible punishment. The second thought shows that she is most concerned about breaking your heart, most likely because the relationship has been nurtured and developed into something that she values and does not want to damage.

It's a small but significant difference.

What have you done to reach and then to maintain your daughter's heart? Whatever you are doing, you probably need to do some more. And you can't ever stop.

WHAT YOUR GIRL WANTS TO TELL YOU

Regarding the vital need for dad's unconditional love, we asked the young women we know about what they wished they would have told their fathers during their teen years. Here's what they said about the importance of the father/daughter relationship. As with all of the other quotes we have snuck into this book, we encourage you to hear these from your daughter's voice:

"I really need consistency in your love."

"Dad, you won't have control over me forever. If I choose a path that isn't what you dreamed up for me, I need you to keep affirming and celebrating God's unique call on my life."

"Use your words to communicate unconditional love. Then treat me in a way that backs it up. When I make a big mistake, I need you to affirm that you still love me."

"When you have a royal dad screw up, quickly make it right. Don't put it off."

"I'm going to change and evolve. Meet me where

I am, no matter where that might be."

"There are a lot of things I can be successful in beyond the tangibles like grades and sports. Affirm little things in my character that have worth. Celebrate the small things."

"Communicate that I am sufficient. Period. God said that He was pleased with Jesus even before He did anything. I need you to do likewise."

Better than just hearing from these girls, ask your daughter if she knows and feels how much you love her. Ask her if there are times when she feels like your love is dependent upon her performance or her behavior. Remind her of your unconditional love and then ask her what you can do to make sure she is more aware of it and secure in it.

Just as our God shows us a relentless, passionate, never-ending love, your daughter needs to feel that from you. In every way that God demonstrates his love for you, you can demonstrate that same kind of love to your girl. As you walk with Jesus, He will show you what your daughter needs from her dad, and He will empower you to give it to her.

MAKE A CLEAR COMMITMENT

We called this book "Meet Me in the Middle" because we feel it takes work to keep a father and daughter connected. It requires you to move out of your comfort zone into her world and it requires her to do the same. We hope that you have found that middle ground through some of the

conversations you have had.

Our hope and prayer is that the lines of communication will stay open between the two of you throughout your lives. With that in mind, we invite you to conclude this experience by making a commitment to God and to each other.

Turn over to page 103 to find the "suitable for framing" promise to your daughter. Since it will be something you give to her, carefully cut it out of the book. (Cut as deep into the margin as you can so that you can trim it and fit it into a 5X7 frame.) Sign your name at the bottom, and give it to your daughter as a pledge of your unconditional love for her. If you want, write a personal note on the back of what will go in the frame (page 104). She won't see the personal note every day, but it will serve as a valuable keepsake to her in the future.

Be sure to give her a big hug when you give it to her. And take your time with it. You want her to always feel loved and safe in your arms.

After all, that's what dads are for.

A Word From the Authors:

If working through this book with your girl has been a good thing in your relationship with her, we would love to hear your story. Take a minute to tell us more about it and to give a little bit of help and encouragement to other dads and daughters at www.facebook.com/MeetMeintheMiddleBook/